THE WASHINGTON PAPERS
Volume V

44: DETENTE AND CONFLICT:
Soviet Foreign Policy
1972-1977

Dimitri K. Simes

THE CENTER FOR STRATEGIC AND INTERNATIONAL STUDIES
Georgetown University, Washington, D.C.

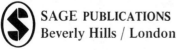

SAGE PUBLICATIONS
Beverly Hills / London

For information address:

SAGE PUBLICATIONS, INC.
275 South Beverly Drive
Beverly Hills, California 90212

SAGE PUBLICATIONS LTD
St George's House / 44 Hatton Garden
London EC1N 8ER

International Standard Book Number 0-8039-0793-1

Library of Congress Catalog Card No. 77-78962

FIRST PRINTING

When citing a Washington Paper, please use the proper form. Remember to cite the series title and include the paper number. One of the two following formats can be adapted (depending on the style manual used):

(1) HASSNER, P. (1973) "Europe in the Age of Negotiation." The Washington Papers, I, 8. Beverly Hills and London: Sage Pubns.

OR

(2) Hassner, Pierre. 1973. *Europe in the Age of Negotiation.* The Washington Papers, vol. 1, no. 8. Beverly Hills and London: Sage Publications.

CONTENTS

AUTHOR'S PREFACE

I am indebted to the following colleagues who took the time to read the manuscript and make valuable suggestions: Ray S. Cline; CSIS; Robert Ivanov, Institute of World History in Moscow; Ernest Lefever, Georgetown University; and Thomas Wolfe of the RAND Corporation. My special appreciation goes to Heidi Kunz and Mira Lansky, my research assistants, who were most helpful. I am solely responsible for the views expressed and the accuracy of factual information.

—Dimitri K. Simes

I. INTRODUCTION

Detente: A Current Assessment

For several years the subject of detente has stirred major controversy in the United States. Commentators have devised a plethora of differing, sometimes mutually exclusive, interpretations of the Soviet Union's actions and intentions. Obviously, the domestic politics as well as the political and ideological preconceptions of the participants in this great debate strongly affect their views. But probably even more important are the ambiguities and contradictions of Soviet foreign policy, which leave it open to conflicting interpretations. In fact, the search for stability and expansionism, cooperation and hostility, activism and caution is an integral part of the modern Soviet attitude toward international relations. The question is not whether Soviet foreign policy includes these elements — for there is sufficient evidence that it does — but rather how heavily each weighs on Soviet activities in the world political arena.

The contradictions in Soviet foreign policy reflect the conflicting interests of the Soviet Union as a rising superpower with a global reach that nonetheless lacks an adequately strong economic posture. They also reflect the paradox of an increasingly conservative, noninnovative regime whose international interests and ideology call for the support of revolutionary movements abroad. The Soviet Union wants many things from the West, both political and economic, but for a number of reasons its leadership feels compelled to indulge in a bitter rivalry with its would-be partners in detente.

The Chinese question also plays a role in Soviet foreign policy decisions. In the nineteenth century it was said that there was a woman behind every political conflict. According to the general wisdom of our times, women have been more or less successfully replaced by oil. Yet even oil pales in comparison to the Soviet competition with Peking, which bears on Moscow's policies in relations with many regions of the world, from the United States to Angola.

The Soviet government is trying simultaneously to improve its domestic economic situation and to become equal if not superior to the United States militarily; to keep its communist allies in line and to establish new strongholds in the world; to prevent a U.S.-Chinese rapprochement and to compete with the United States for global political influence; to undermine the power of West European governments and to obtain from them much-needed credits and technology; to support the producers of oil and other raw materials against the industrial nations and to deny the conservative oil-rich states like Saudi Arabia stronger positions in the third world. This multiplicity of conflicting interests virtually assures inconsistencies and ambiguities in Soviet foreign policy. The Kremlin has had to establish a list of priorities, since it is often necessary to make sacrifices in one area in order to achieve successes in another. This list is not static. New developments — a disastrous harvest or the American president's visit to Peking — can at least temporarily change the Soviet leadership's international priorities, as in fact has happened on numerous occasions.

Still, it is possible to extrapolate some of the fundamental interests behind Soviet foreign policy. Most important is to assure the security of the Soviet state, both as a territorial and social entity. The preservation of the existing political system is viewed by Moscow as a fundamental security requirement. The Soviet notion of security comprises both permanent and changing elements. On the permanent side is the search for absolute security. For both historical and psychological reasons the leadership is not ready to settle for anything less than reliable protection against all potential foreign and domestic challenges. "Of course, comrades, we are perfecting our defenses. It cannot be otherwise. We have never sacrificed and will never sacrifice the security of our country, the security of our allies," General Secretary Leonid I. Brezhnev stated recently (Pravda, 1977g).

But how does Moscow define security? Total security is impossible in the nuclear age. Whether the Kremlin will acknowledge this impossibility, or whether it will embark on an endless drive for overwhelming superiority over all real and potential adversaries cannot be answered simply. The evidence suggests, however, that current Soviet leadership feels threatened by hostile international force it cannot control. As the U.S.S.R. becomes a global power its definition of security expands and becomes more complex. No longer is it confined to security for the Soviet mainland; it also includes protecting allies and friends, the positions of Soviet forces stationed abroad, Soviet military and naval bases outside the U.S.S.R., and to some degree, even access to international ocean lines of communication.

The Soviet government uses both cooperation and conflict as policy tools to preserve security in its new expanded version. From the official standpoint both are integral elements of detente. According to Brezhnev (Pravda, 1977g):

> Detente means first of all overcoming the Cold War and then a transition to normal, stable relations among states. Detente means the willingness to resolve differences and disputes not by force, not by threats and saber-rattling, but by peaceful means at the conference table. Detente means a certain trust and the ability to consider each other's legitimate interests.

The Soviet leadership is responsible enough to realize that unrestrained and uncontrolled hostility could lead to a holocaust. It is also pragmatic enough to see that in many instances cooperation with the West can confer tangible political and economic advantages on the U.S.S.R., thus enhancing Soviet national security. A good example is SALT, which in the Soviet view serves to restrain American strategic programs and helps to control nuclear rivalry. Similarly, detente between the U.S.S.R. and France, and even more important between the U.S.S.R. and West Germany assures the Kremlin that its domination over Eastern Europe will not be challenged by the West.

But a committment to cooperate with the West when there exists a coincidence of interests has never meant that the Soviet Union would refrain from hostile activities when it feels its security interests are endangered. The tough response to Western, particularly American, efforts to support Soviet dissidents persecuted and harassed by the authorities illustrates this point. The history of the regime reveals that because considerations of political security for the Soviet system take precedence over everything else, no "carrot and stick" the West could use would result in substantive changes in the system itself. The Soviet definition of security is based on the assumption of the legitimacy of the Soviet regime. Recognition of this legitimacy is perceived as the minimal requirement for those who seek constructive relations with Moscow. As George Kennan (1976) rightly observes:

> In this complicated world there could be no international relationship

which was one of total antagonism or total identity of interests — none which did not contain both sorts of ingredients, however uneven the mix.

The Soviet leadership accepts and, as a matter of fact, constantly articulates that detente is not a love affair, but simply the ability "to take into consideration each other's legitimate interests."

It does not seem, however, that from the Soviet standpoint there can be any compromise when the most fundamental security interests are involved. In this sense detente is widely perceived as a shield to protect the Soviet state and its clients. In no way does the Kremlin interpret detente as authorization for the West to interfere in Soviet domestic affairs or to exert greater influence in Soviet-dominated Eastern Europe.

Certainly the Kremlin's foreign policy in general, and detente with the West in particular, stem from interests reaching far beyond mere security considerations. The U.S.S.R. has recently engaged in superpower meddling, which possibly not only feeds some more or less marginal Soviet interests but also appeals to Russian pride. The regime is determined not to miss any opportunity to improve its international position, even at the expense of its partners in detente. At the same time it hopes that detente can play a role in attracting Western investment in Soviet economic development. All of these motivations behind Soviet foreign policy are far from unimportant, but in these areas — unlike security — compromises are considered possible. Obviously, Soviet willingness to compromise depends upon whether there is a realistic chance to achieve desirable objectives without making unpleasant concessions. But in this sense the Soviet policy makers are far from unique.

What is really unique about Soviet foreign policy is that it is rooted in the conviction that time definitely works in Moscow's favor. When Soviet leaders declare that their country is involved in a major "peaceful offensive," they mean what they say. It seems that the primary obstacle in relations between the two superpowers is not so much the difference between their political and social systems, although this is a serious factor, but rather the incompatibility of their objectives on the international scene. The United States views itself basically as a status quo power. American involvement abroad remains stable in some areas and is being reduced in others. In accepting detente, U.S. policy makers seek a more secure and stable world. The Soviets are comfortable with the first objective because they share the view that nuclear war must be avoided and that mutual restraint and careful management of crisis situations are vital in the period of rough strategic parity. Unlike the Americans, however, the Russians are not committed to international stability. They believe that they are riding the crest of historical trends and that the world's balance of power is shifting in their favor.

As a result, there are natural limits to progress in relations with Russia, limits which have to be realistically appreciated if these relations are to be stable and mutually advantageous. While detente appears to have survived the troubled events of the recent past, these developments have served to define more clearly its real meaning, which is not always in accord with the norms of conduct prescribed by the Soviet-American summit communiques. If detente is expected to institute a new era of stability and cooperation, accompanied by a degree of democratization of Soviet society, it cannot succeed. If, however, it is defined simply as an attempt by both superpowers to control their rivalry when their interests diverge, and to cooperate to their mutual advantage when their interests more or less coincide, then detente can accomplish as much today as during the first summit in Moscow.

Detente can and should modify the rules and operational principles of the superpower rivalry, but it cannot change the name of the game. At best it can end the zero-sum approach to relations between the United States and the Soviet Union, and convince the Soviet leadership that an American loss does not necessarily equal a Soviet gain — a modest goal still far from being assured. Meanwhile, the Soviet Union and the United States will continue to be major adversaries on the international scene for a long period to come.

To be sure, detente comprises only one among many dimensions of the superpowers' international activities. Granted that the United States and the Soviet Union serve as restraining forces on each other, it nevertheless remains doubtful that the Russians consider the relationship, or even relations with the West in general, as a pivotal salient of their foreign policy. Significantly, in recent years the Kremlin has found it easier to deal with the United States than with many traditional and new centers of power, particularly China and the Arab countries. Simultaneously, developments in the third world, and currently in Western Europe, furnish greater opportunities for Moscow to improve its international position than contacts with the United States, no matter how profitable. This diversity of Soviet foreign policy interests, some of them incompatible with the requirements of the Soviet-American relationship, inevitably imposes additional limitations on detente.

Moreover, the domestic roots of Soviet foreign policy do not allow for real accommodation with the "imperialist enemy." The Soviet leadership must carefully weigh the benefits of relaxation in relations with the West against the dangers and challenges it poses to a totalitarian society. Currently, Marxist-Leninist ideology does not offer any operational guidance to Soviet policy makers, but is used extensively to justify numerous unattractive features of the regime both at home and abroad. In this sense, the ideology stil plays an important role. Without an external enemy the Kremlin would be hard put to explain to its own people the rigid political controls, the absense of the most elementary democratic freedoms, and the constant shortages of consumer goods. A further consequence of the frequent invocation of Marxism-Leninism is that it forces pragmatic members of the top command to live according to their pronouncements, thus making them prisoners of an ideology they do not necessarily take all that seriously.

The imposition of certain limits on detente or the recognition of its "natural" limits does not endanger the modicum of international cooperation that prevails at present; rather it helps to ensure it by discarding illusionary aspects and retaining essential and more promising ones. The more inflated the expectations of detente, particularly with regard to internal or domestic reforms, the greater the danger that it will not survive the inevitable disillusionment and frustration. This danger almost materialized during the 1976 election campaign and, as the controversy over Soviet political repression testifies, it still persists. The world would be more secure if we could learn to coexist and even cooperate with expansionist dictatorial regimes without either misplaced warmth or unwarranted hatred and fear. Avoiding the two extremes will not be easy. It requires a cold approach in a society known for its search for absolutes. But finding the balance between the desirable and the possible is what a coherent foreign policy is all about.

II. CONTINUITY AND CHANGE IN SOVIET FOREIGN POLICY

The Soviet View of Detente: From Lenin to Brezhnev

In May 1972, President Richard Nixon arrived in Moscow for summit talks with Leonid Brezhnev and other Soviet leaders. This summit is usually designated as the beginning of U.S.-Soviet detente. Addressing a joint session of Congress upon his return home, Nixon (U.S. Dept. of State, 1973: 613) spoke about the "opportunity to build a new structure of peace in the world." Nevertheless, the American president cautiously reminded his audience that "Soviet ideology still proclaims hostility to some of America's most basic values. The Soviet leaders remain committed to that ideology. Like the nation they lead, they are and they will continue to be, totally dedicated competitors of the United States of America." Despite this important qualifying statement, the jubilant tone of the address and many speeches to follow often suggested a much more far-reaching achievement than the substantive results of the Soviet-American rapprochement could justify.

Overstating the progress of detente, however, was not entirely an American phenomenon. In Moscow, the newspapers toned down their criticism of the United States, including the American involvement in Vietnam. The summit was widely portrayed as an event of historical significance, a "fundamental transformation of international relations."

Little was said about the conditions that made these developments possible. The hopes were too high, the fabric of the new U.S.-Soviet relationship too delicate to allow for such discussion. The continuing combat in Vietnam naturally precluded excessive optimism about the future of U.S.-Soviet relations on the part of Soviet commentators. But one point was made continuously: the Soviet Union had always desired peaceful coexistence with the West, especially the United States. Consequently the summit marked a triumph for the "peace-loving" Soviet foreign policy.

In a way, what Soviet officials and commentators were saying reflected their true feelings. America has always occupied a special place in Soviet foreign policy thinking. The Soviet leadership, has habitually measured its position in the world by comparing it with that of the United States. Khrushchev in his memoirs (1974: 374) becomes almost sentimental when he describes his 1959 visit to the most powerful capitalist country. "We were proud," he told Soviet leaders on his return, "that we had finally forced the United States to recognize the necessity to establish closer contacts with us. If the President of the United States himself invites the Chairman of the Council of Ministers of the U.S.S.R., then you know conditions have changed. We have come a long way from the time when the United States wouldn't even grant us diplomatic recognition." In 1959 the Soviet Union was clearly the weaker of the two great powers, and Khrushchev, as he indicates in his memoirs, knew that very well. By 1972 Moscow could credit the summit for having given it something it had never received, but greatly desired for both practical and symbolic reasons: formal recognition as a superpower second to none.

From the Soviet standpoint this landmark in the drive for parity with America was reached primarily because of the new, more favorable balance of forces in the international arena. Detente did not seem to result so much from mutual restraint and the end of unlimited mutual hostility as from growing Soviet power and international influence. Alterations in the U.S.-Soviet relationship were hardly expected to change this trend because, from the very beginning, detente with the West also meant detente against the West.

Razryadka, the Russian equivalent of *detente*, is a relatively new word in the Soviet political vocabulary. But Soviet governments since the early days of the Bolshevik state have spoken about peaceful coexistence with the noncommunist world, and with the United States in particular. Originally, Lenin and his lieutenants felt that the Russian Revolution could survive only if it was supported by similar revolutions in major Western countries. Since such revolutions did not materialize and the young Bolshevik regime was not strong enough to overthrow West

European governments by force, peaceful coexistence with the hostile capitalist environment was accepted as an integral part of Soviet foreign policy strategy.

From the start, the Bolsheviks especially hoped to normalize their relationship with the United States. First, they considered the United States the strongest of their capitalist adversaries, both economically and politically. More contacts and trade with the rising Western power could enormously benefit the communist regime. Second, the top command was realistic enough to understand that while there was some remote chance for revolution in Europe, which inherited economic difficulties and political instability from the First World War, there was no such possibility in the United States. Thus, the Soviet leaders had no choice but to find some form of long-term accommodation with America, with characteristic pragmatism they wanted to make it as profitable for themselves as possible.

As early as 1918 Lenin tried to convince his American visitors that friendship and trade were in the interest of both countries (Sbornik Leninskiy XXXVII, 1970: 254). In December 1919, in an interview with *The Christian Science Monitor* (1975) he suggested a need to reach economic agreement and emphasized the inevitability of "coexistence side by side" of the capitalist and socialist systems. Several months later Lenin (1941: 145) pledged peace with "American capitalists" and offered Russian gold and raw materials in return for American machinery. His death did not change the government's interest in developing an economic relationship with the United States, and by 1930 the United States was the primary Soviet economic partner (Mezhdunarodnaya Zhizn, 1974).

Certainly there were ups and downs in contacts between the communist regime in Moscow and the United States. Furthermore, the Soviet interpretation of Lenin's peaceful coexistence slogan was frequently adjusted to the practical requirements of Soviet foreign policy. Nevertheless, at every stage of the relationship the Kremlin tried to turn existing opportunities to its greatest advantage, whether it was during World War II in the period when the countries were allied, or the first two postwar decades when they were bitter adversaries.

Krushchev revitalized the slogan of peaceful coexistence, but at the same time promised to bury the American political system. The current Soviet "peaceful offensive" was initiated by Brezhnev and his Politburo associates. At first, like Lenin and Khrushchev, they used the term *peaceful coexistence*, but as their connections with the West grew, *razryadka* was used more and more frequently. Interestingly, the Russian word *razryadka* and the French word *detente* have similar meanings from a linguistic point of view. The verb *razryadit* literally means to discharge a weapon. *Detente* derives from slackening the bowstring of a crossbow. In a sense, detente in Russian connotes "close to a thaw." There is something temporary and unstable about these processes. Detente, razryadka, does not mean destruction of weapons or even ammunition. Whether it involves anything more than removing bullets from a gun, permanently or temporarily, remains to be seen.

It would be an oversimplification to portray the Soviet policy of detente as nothing more than a deceptive tactical maneuver. To the Russians the period between the Bolshevik Revolution and World War II and the Cold War years hardly represent an ideal model for relations with the West. Revisionist historians make too much of Soviet grievances, many of which were essentially self-inflicted. But there remains the fact that for decades the U.S.S.R. had to struggle for mere survival. Whether or not its political survival was in the best interests of the world and Soviet citizenry is another question. What matters here is that those running the affairs of the U.S.S.R. viewed Western behavior as a threat to their very existence, and often insult was added to injury. For years the Soviet Union was treated as a second-class citizen on the international scene. Those who criticize the West's harsh approach to Moscow in the prewar period often err by looking at the U.S.S.R. of the twenties and thirties through the prism of our assessment of the Soviet Union in the seventies.[1] During the first two postrevolutionary decades it remained a second-class power with an unbelievably cruel and repressive regime and doubtful domestic stability. Its political system was an unknown quantity without parallels in history, one that looked so unnatural and so contrary to the values of Western civilization that it inevitably prompted the belief that it could not last for long.

The limited Western intervention in Russia during its civil war was never intended to overthrow the Bolshevik regime by force. At best it could have afforded some marginal assistance to the White armies. Nevertheless, it proved to Lenin and his associates that the West was fundamentally hostile toward their rule. Lenin, and later Stalin, always stated that the only reason the West did not intervene on a larger scale was because Western workers had tired of World War I and were basically sympathetic to the objectives of the revolution.

The Soviet leaders even interpreted America's generous relief during the devastating post-civil war famine as a humiliation. It implied that their country was too weak to function without the assistance of Western capitalists, whom in principle they preferred to see "eliminated as a class." During the early twenties Lenin's New Economic Policy attracted Western investments but he and his immediate successors felt politically threatened and isolated by the hostile "capitalist encirclement." These fears were fed in the thirties by the suspicion the West wanted to use Hitler as a tool to destroy the Soviet system. Munich, and the apparent unwillingness of the West to cooperate wholeheartedly with the Soviet communists against the Nazis, only aggravated suspicions. After the war both Stalin and the regime as a whole were appalled to find the West challenging their domination of Eastern Europe, which they considered vital protection from future invasions. Furthermore, the Soviet Union, which had defeated Germany at enormous sacrifice, once again felt threatened militarily. This vulnerability was exacerbated by U.S. development of the atomic bomb.

In the late forties and the fifties, the Soviets were threatened first with containment, and then with liberation. They read about bomber and missile gaps in their favor, while in fact suffering tremendous strategic inferiority. The open encouragement by Radio Free Europe of the uprising in Hungary served as another reminder of Western hostility.

The Cuban missile crisis of the early sixties supplied the impetus for a major Soviet strategic buildup. Why Khrushchev decided to install Soviet missiles in Cuba remains something of a mystery. Some experts, such as Adam Ulam (1976: 152), believe that most likely "those Soviet missiles in Cuba were to be used as a bargaining chip." He argues that "had the United States agreed to a German treaty and, perhaps also to a nuclear free zone in the Pacific, the missiles would have been withdrawn." I suspect that while the missiles were supposed to be utilized primarily as a political instrument, they were also intended to serve ambitious military goals. Because the United States enjoyed superiority in ICBMs and strategic bombers and commanded bases on the periphery of Soviet territory, the Kremlin judged itself far more vulnerable to an American nuclear strike than the United States to a Soviet strike. Deploying Soviet missiles in Cuba was possibly a desperate effort to redress this unfavorable balance. The effort failed. But in Soviet eyes it failed not because Moscow had erred, but because it was the weaker of the two parties (Khrushchev, 1974: 512-514; see also Newhouse, 1973: 68).

By listing these Soviet complaints about the earlier stages of coexistence with the West, I do not mean to suggest that Moscow was treated unfairly. Even at that time the Soviets generally managed to get the better part of the bargain. Their behavior was frequently ugly and inexcusable. In many cases their fears were so paranoid that nobody could take them seriously. As a result, the West's lack of respect for the Soviet Union can be primarily attributed to Soviet actions at home and abroad. Nevertheless, if one does not take the earlier frustrations into account it is impossible to understand Moscow's attitude toward detente.

In the decades before Stalin's death, Soviet leaders were not ready to accept any form of accommodation with the West, even if it might prove profitable. They were forced to make an exception during World War II, when the alternative to an alliance with the Western democracies could well have been a military defeat and the destruction of the Soviet political system. All other temporary thaws in East-West relations were short-term marriages of convenience without deep roots. Moscow's insecurity would not allow for anything more.

While great, the U.S.S.R. remained primarily a local power until the late sixties. It did not concern itself much with developments in remote regions or even Western Europe, but rather with cementing controls over the newly acquired Soviet empire, both inside and outside its official borders. In addition, the Kremlin was not powerful enough to deal with the West as an equal and did not want to negotiate from a position of weakness, particularly at a time when the NATO allies expressed reluctance to recognize the Soviet domination in Eastern Europe and the Far East as a political reality. In the economic field, the Soviet Union hoped that cooperation with its client states would be sufficient to assure rapid growth of its own economy. To appeal to the West for massive economic assistance was unthinkable. Domestically, the regime under both Stalin and Khrushchev maintained rigid totalitarian controls over the populace: exchanges of information and even culture with the noncommunist world were considered practically out of the question. Khrushchev's totalitarian policies were undoubtedly less repressive and merciless than those of Stalin. Yet no dissent was permitted and no ideas or initiatives emanated from outside the party and state institutional structure. In many ways, Khrushchev ruled more dictatorially and intolerantly than any of his successors.

The Cold War was convenient for the Russian leaders when they felt insecure both at home and abroad, and the Soviet international position was more uncertain than it is today. They used the Cold War mainly as a defensive political strategy to consolidate their power against both Western adversaries and potential domestic opponents, who might take advantage of the instability and uncertainty created by Stalin's death to question their supreme authority. Unlike the Cold War, detente is an activist offensive strategy. It was developed by a regime confident of its international stature, a regime which believes that it has achieved rough strategic parity with its major rival, the United States, and has learned that domestic dissent, if kept within certain limits, does not represent a threat to the established social and political order.

Serious new problems nevertheless confront the Kremlin. Conflict with China and the growing independence of some East European states undermine its control over the communist bloc. The top command not only fears being pressed from two flanks, the Far East and Western Europe, but is also engaged in an international rivalry with Peking. From 1969 to 1973, an American-Chinese rapprochement directed against the Soviet Union was considered a real threat. At that time, some Soviet think tanks organized military games to ascertain how the West might react to a Soviet preventive nuclear strike against Chinese nuclear and other military installations, possibly followed by occupation of parts of China. Simultaneously, Soviet scholars visiting the United States persisted with questions about similar exercises taking place in American academic institutions. Later, evidently because of the lack of rapid progress in relations between Washington and Peking, Soviet concern diminished s omewhat, but it has never completely disappeared. The conflict with China deeply troubled the Soviet leaders and resulted in a complete reevaluation of Soviet foreign policy strategy. Normalization with the West, and the United states in particular, formed an integral part of this policy review.

The economic difficulties of the Soviet Union — and primarily its obvious inability to combine totalitarianism with rational administration of its economy — also exerted pressure toward normalization with the West. In the late sixties, the Soviets tried to achieve a selective detente with Western Europe, but it worked neither economically nor politically. The governments of the European NATO members, including France, hesitated to change the nature of their relations with the Soviet Union beyond the level of rhetoric and atmospherics without participation by the United States. Consequently, the Soviets could not obtain the credits and technolgy they desired, failing some positive movement in the Soviet-American relationship.

The gradual loss of the Soviet lead to the United States in space exploration — the only branch of technological competition in which the U.S.S.R. had succeeded in temporarily seizing superficial superiority — confirmed the significance of economic and technological cooperation with the West to the Soviet leadership. The outcome of the military competition with the United States was clearly at stake. The fact that maintaining social stability within the Soviet Union depended to a certain degree on the availability of a sufficient quantity of consumer goods and food also played a subordinate role in convincing Soviet leaders of the value of U.S.-Soviet cooperation. No matter how reluctantly, the Soviet Union had to accept a degree of dependency on the West, and, in particular, the United States.

A detailed interpretation of the factors that made detente possible is set forth in several articles by academician Georgiy A. Arbatov (1974, 1973a), director of the prestigious Soviet Institute of the United States and Canada and an adviser to Brezhnev. He singles out revisions in the United States political position rather than changes in basic Soviet policies. Like all other Soviet politicians, academics, and publicists, Arbatov designates as foremost among these factors the shift of the "correlation of forces in the world arena" in favor of the Soviet Union and its allies. In his words, "in the final analysis, it is precisely this which compelled the capitalist world after protracted and bitter opposition to acknowledge the changes that have taken place as a result of socialist revolutions on a considerable portion of the globe." Arbatov also gives special credit to the strenghening of the Soviet military for preventing the United States from being able to use military means to exert political pressure. In addition, he cites the "peace-loving" course of the Soviet leadership, the so-called "peaceful offensive," as one of the more important reasons for detente. Finally, he and many other Soviet observers call attention to the awareness "of a considerable part of the United States' ruling circles" that the new correlation of forces will even frequently rule out local wars as a tool of "imperialist strategy."

Arbatov's arguments appear to amount to more than propagandistic word-mongering. Indeed, if divested of ideological labels, they make sense, particularly since he indirectly admits that Soviet policy did not remain completely unchanged. While the Soviet Union has pursued a "consistent peace-loving foreign policy" since the revolution, Arbatov states that the peaceful offensive was intensified in recent years as a direct result of decisions made at the Twenty-fourth Congress of the Soviet Communist Party in 1971. Irrespective of one's view of how peace-loving Soviet policy actually was or is, one can agree with Arbatov that sometime around 1971 the current shape of the Soviet policy of detente was designed.

According to conventional U.S. wisdom, Moscow became interested in detente with the United States primarily because it needed American technology and credits and feared that American-Chinese rapprochement would be directed against the Soviet Union. The Soviets emphatically reject this point of view. They have frequently announced that there is simply no reasonable alternative to detente in the nuclear age. Curiously enough there is every reason to believe that they mean what they say. Despite the Soviet government's refusal to accept the 1972 trade agreement with the United States, and evidence of lessened concern about a Washington-Peking axis, it is clear that Moscow still desires (possibly more than ever before) to continue its detente policy.

The depth and stability of Soviet interest in detente have frequently been seriously underestimated. While the Chinese factor and the troubles of the Soviet economy could significantly enhance the appeal of detente, several important factors, some totally unrelated to U.S. behavior, currently account for its continuing strong commitment. Particularly prominent are Soviet desires to influence domestic situations in Western countries, to codify the arms race according to Soviet needs and capabilities. to improve the Soviet image abroad, to strengthen Soviet positions in the third world, and to weaken Western resistance to Soviet global political activism. The Soviets rightly believe that under the Circumstances of mutual deterrence, detente has become an optimal vehicle to promote their foreign policy interests. It is precisely from this perspective that Soviet spokesmen do not see any reasonable alternative to detente. Soviet foreign policy, including strategy toward communist, nationalist, and left-wing movements, is based solidly on detente. Consequently, it would take much more than an unfriendly American gesture or a tough stand on an important issue to convince Moscow to abandon detente in favor of another foreign policy strategy. Even then, such a shift would likely create tension between the Soviet Union and some of its East European allies, as well as Soviet clients among West European communist parties.

As long as the present balance of power is preserved, Soviet foreign policy is likely to be based on detente. The committment to detente could only be abandoned if the Kremlin felt that it had achieved significant superiority over the United States as a result of its military buildup and U.S. unilateral restraint and/or because of international economic, political, and military developments unfavorable to the American position in the world. Otherwise, a little more or a little less detente will emanate from Moscow, but the core of the policy will remain intact.

From Cairo to Luanda
with Stops in Saigon and Lisbon

The unmaking of detente as it was perceived by the majority of the U.S. public, the Congress, and the media probably began in October 1973, when the United States and the Soviet Union supported opposing sides in the Arab-Israeli conflict. Afterward, Moscow's attempts to influence Portuguese developments, its role in the collapse of South Vietnam, and finally its intervention in Angola through the use of Cuban proxies further dampened American overoptimism about detente. But the problem derived from misperceptions about detente rather than from the process itself. The Soviet government never represented it as a reconciliation of the two systems. Detente was supposed to codify the superpower rivalry, if possible to complement it with some elements of cooperation, but not to change its competitive nature.

Even in its earlier stages, Soviet statements about detente were self-explanatory. Before the Yom Kippur War, Georgiy Arbatov (1973a), who is generally regarded as a moderate by Soviet standards, said that "the struggle between socialism and capitalism is historically inevitable." Nikolay V. Podgorny, Politburo member and Supreme Soviet Presidium chairman, explained (Pravda, 1973a):

> As the Soviet people see it, a just and democratic world cannot be achieved without the national and social liberation of peoples. The struggle by the Soviet Union for the relaxation of international tensions, for peaceful coexistence among states with different systems does not represent, and cannot represent, a departure from the class principles of our foreign policy.

Statements like these were well known to western experts and media commentators, but were dismissed as propaganda designed both for domestic political purposes and as a rebuttal to Chinese charges of a superpower conspiracy.

During his 1967-1972 tenure with the Soviet Institute of World Economy and International Relations in Moscow, this writer witnessed and on a few occasions participated in discussions about the nature of the new relationships with the West. Significantly, almost none of the foreign policy experts and Central Committee officials who visited the Institute perceived detente as marking an end to the Soviet Union's historic struggle with the West. They considered it necessary to shed some of the old myths that depicted the Western community as an international evil rather than as an objective adversary. They agreed that total war should be avoided and that cooperation with the West in certain areas would be desirable,but that the struggle for world influence will continue to be an integral element of Soviet strategy in the future. In their view the world was changing and would continue to change in ways favorable to Soviet interests, and that the task of detente is "to insure" that these changes take as painless a form as possible. [2] Thus, detente was, and still is, seen by the Soviet leadership, including the more moderate factions, as the most effective way for the Soviet Union to alter the international status quo without risking a major conflict with the United States.

The Soviet government does recognize, however, that detente entails compromise and mutual restraint. In Cuba, Vietnam, the Middle East, Portugal, and to some extent even Angola, the U.S.S.R. has displayed a degree of caution in order to avoid a collision with the West, and not jeopardize detente. Soviet behavior in these crises did not coincide with Western interests, but it could hardly be called irresponsible. As a matter of fact, on each of these occasions Russia went almost as far and as fast as it could go without provoking a major increase in international tension.

There were some miscalculations: Angola is a case in point. But generally speaking, if the U.S.S.R. continues to go too far too fast — as many observers in the West feel it does — the blame should be shared by those who allow it do so without fear of reprisals. The Soviet Politburo may be guilty of many things, but it is hardly responsible for the lack of will, strategic purpose, and unity of the Western nations. As former Secretary of State Henry Kissinger (U.S. Dept. of State, 1975) put it:

> What we cannot ask the Soviet Union to do is to keep itself from taking advantage of situations in which, for whatever reasons, we do not do what is required to maintain the balance. It is true that Soviet arms made the conquest of South Vietnam possible. It is also true that the refusal of American arms made the conquest of South Vietnam inevitable.

Fearful of appearing to be weak, Moscow resents any linkage between its behavior in crisis situations and other aspects of detente (Zhurkin, 1975: 277). Indeed, if the West were to publicize linkage it could humiliate the Soviet leaders. It would also prove counterproductive because despite their failure to acknowledge that fact, the leaders have clearly tempered their actions on the basis of an awareness of linkage.

There are other factors at work that receive priority over the Soviet interest in detente. The regime has quite a few problems, of which the Chinese factor is the most pressing. Most Soviet actions on the international scene cannot be properly understood if the Sino-Soviet dispute is not taken into account. In addition, the U.S.S.R. has numerous allies and clients who lobby for its causes. Since it has not fared well in uncongenial areas, the leadership cannot take many of these countries for granted. Frequently, their demands are difficult to ignore because Peking would be only too happy to exploit any differences between the Soviets and developing countries. This enables many recipients of Soviet aid to gain important leverage over the U.S.S.R. North Vietnam, for instance, for years skillfully manipulated the Sino-Soviet rivalry to its own benefit. Determined to avoid pushing the North Vietnamese into China's embrace, the Kremlin was reluctant to apply any political pressure on them.

Even if there were no conflict with China, Moscow would still try to extract advantages from opportunities periodically emerging in areas of political instability as long as this would not lead to a direct confrontation with the West. Brezhnev was quite outspoken on this point when he addressed the Twenty-Fifth Party Congress in the aftermath of the Angolan crisis (Pravda, 1976c):

> It is a constant principle of our Leninist foreign policy to respect the sacred right of every people, every country, to choose its own way of development. But we do not conceal our views. In the developing countries, as everywhere else, we are on the side of the forces of progress, democracy and national independence, and regard them as friends and comrades in struggle. Our party supports and will continue to support peoples fighting for their freedom.

According to Brezhnev, "detente does not in the slightest way abolish or alter the laws of the class struggle. No one should expect that because of detente Communists will reconcile themselves to capitalist exploitation or that monopolists will become followers of the revolution."

The Soviet approach to international crises includes the following major elements: first, the Soviet Union does not export revolution where conditions are unfavorable; second, it supports leftist and nationalist "anti-imperialist" forces outside its sphere of influence; third, such support is provided in areas where the Soviets believe there are opportunities to score gains without provoking a major international confrontation. Since even the most conservative anticommunist regimes are considered anti-imperialist once they ally themselves with the Soviet Union, virtually every country or political movement hostile to the United States and/or to Peking can rely to some degree on Soviet support. In the early sixties, Khrushchev awarded Nasser the title of "Hero of the Soviet Union," depite the fact that the late Egyptian dictator had jailed hundreds of native communists. In 1975, disappointed by Egyptian President Sadat's drift to the West, the Soviets improved relations with Libya's Qaddafi, a militant anticommunist who had frequently been attacked by the Soviet state-controlled media. The Kremlin intended to use Quaddafi as a restraining force on Sadat.

Soviet involvement in the political and military conflicts in the Middle East, Vietnam, Portugal, and Angola established certain patterns of behavior in crisis situations, patterns which basically conform to the Kremlin's public statements. These tactics can be described as cautious expansionism; on the one hand, the U.S.S.R. did not forgo any opportunity to improve its international standing at the expense of Washington and Peking; but on the other, it dared not rock the boat too hard.

The October 1973 Middle East war is often considered (Edmonds, 1975: 138) the first test of detente. It came as a shock to most Americans that after all the champagne-drinking in the Kremlin and the White House, after all the declarations about "mutual interdependence," "the structure of peace," and "the era of negotiations," Moscow was headed on a collision course with the United States. From the Soviet standpoint, however, its actions were natural and justified. They were certainly predictable to students of Soviet foreign policy.

Soviet policy in the Middle East had suffered a severe setback. Relations with Egypt were rapidly deteriorating, a process that reached its climax when in July 1972, President Sadat expelled roughly 20,000 Soviet military advisers from the country. Sadat even denied a Soviet request for an eighty-man military mission (Heikal, 1975: 178). Almost overnight the Soviet military and political presence in Egypt plummeted. Moscow was disappointed and bitter because its plan to gradually transform Egypt into a client state had completely failed. And it had failed despite a Soviet investment of major proportions there. Obviously, pragmatic Soviet interests — to make Egypt more dependent on the Soviet Union, to establish Soviet naval facilities in the country, and to avoid another Arab defeat humiliating to the Kremlin — played a principal role in determining Soviet policies. But, a feeling also pervaded Soviet ruling circles that Egypt had not properly appreciated its generous assistance. Not only had it received huge supplies of arms and ammunition, but the Soviets assumed responsibility for Egyptian air defenses, manning Russian-made SAMs and MIG interceptors (Pravda, 1977c). Furthermore, in at least one incident Soviet pilots took part in actual combat, when five MIGs were destroyed by Israeli aircraft (Heikal, 1975: 164).

There was an objective difference between Soviet and Egyptian interests, as is inevitable in dealings between global and local powers. Frequently the Russians tactlessly disregarded Egyptian sensitivities. As Klaus Mehnert (CSIS, 1976: 9) a perceptive observer of Soviet policy, put it, an "ugly Russian" pattern of behavior, which was evident in the Soviet attitude toward Egypt, was to a great extent responsible for Sadat's break with Moscow. Nevertheless, there was another important lesson the Soviet Union had to learn as a rising global power, a lesson the United States had learned many years before: giants are disliked and suspected simply because they are giants, and very little can be done about it.

Despite obvious frustration, the official Soviet reaction was cool and pragmatic. The regime attempted to preserve whatever influence and presence it could still maintain in Egypt. One way of doing so was by increasing arms deliveries. A revealing account of Soviet policy during the period between the expulsion of Soviet military personnel in July 1972, and October 1973, was made by Mohamed Heikal (1975: 183), editor of *Al-Ahram*, an influential Egyptian newspaper:

> The Russians certainly seemed to have recovered themselves sufficiently to adopt new tactics. They seemed anxious to recover lost ground by speeding

up the flow of arms, to such an extent that I remember President Sadat saying to me one day: "They are drowning me in new arms." Between December 1972 and June 1973, we received more arms from them than in the whole of the two preceding years.

The Soviets undoubtedly knew that by supplying arms they were making war between the Arabs and the Israelis and a potential confrontation between the superpowers more likely. But a desire to salvage the remains of the Soviet presence in Egypt prevailed. This desire also narrowed Soviet leverage over Sadat's Israeli policy. It was clear that the Egyptian President would not let Moscow tell him what to do.

In strengthening the Egyptian forces, the Soviet leaders probably reasoned, a limited war in the Middle East could promote their interests, despite the risk of conflict with the United States. First, a resumption of hostilities on a limited scale could again push the Arab states into the Soviet camp. The U.S.S.R., which did not maintain diplomatic relations with Israel, was in no position to deliver an acceptable settlement to the Arabs, but it was the only great power that could and would help them in case of war. Second, there was the need to defend and if possible to improve the Soviet position in the third world. This position was challenged by China and a number of African and Asian countries at the Fourth Summit Conference of Nonaligned Nations in Algeria in September 1973. The superpower conspiracy against the underdeveloped world was one of the favorite topics at that meeting. The third world countries, which for some years had played the superpowers against each other, feared that detente might change the rules of the game. Although Moscow found some satisfaction in the strong defense it received from Fidel Castro, the message was clear: pursued too far, detente might possibly benefit the Soviet positions in Europe, but could boost China in its rivalry with the Soviet Union for leadership in the third world. Something had to be done to improve the Soviet image among the Arabs and their third world friends. Consequently, Walter Laqueur (1974: 81) rightly says, "the Soviet dilemma with regard to the war was not whether it should support it, but how far its involvement could go without unduly antagonizing Western believers in detente."

Still, there is no evidence that the Soviets actually encouraged the Arabs to attack. Moscow simply went along with the decision made in Cairo and Damascus. Moreover, it appears that the Soviet government did not learn about the Arab plans until several days before the attack. Preserving a cautious stance, and possibly assuming an Arab defeat, the Soviets evacuated their personnel from Egypt and Syria two days before the war (Rubinstein, 1974: 27).

Soviet behavior during the 1973 October War should be analyzed on the levels of local conflict in the Middle East and global competition between the superpowers. On the first level, the Soviets were certainly not helpful, but cautious and restrained: they knew about the war in advance and did nothing to prevent it.[3] They also did not tell the United States about the Arab plans, despite the provisions of the 1973 agreement on the prevention of nuclear war which allegedly obliged both parties to advise one another of emerging crisis situations that could develop into nuclear conflicts. But the Soviet Union neither intended to risk a holocaust nor did it consider military confrontation with the United States a real threat. At any rate, would the United States have advised the Soviet Union if the Israelis and not the Arabs had been the first to attack? After all, both Washington and Moscow had pledged that detente in no way eliminated commitments to their allies, and the Soviet Union had agreements with Egypt and Syria. Therefore, from both legal and political points of view, the Soviet   commitment to advise the United States about the coming Arab offensive appears rather ambiguous.

The Soviet Union also initially rejected the idea of a return to the 1967 ceasefire lines, but so did Great Britain and France. Even Secretary of State Kissinger had second thoughts about putting an immediate end to the advance of the Arab armies (Kalb and Kalb, 1975; Laqueur, 1974). Many observers held Moscow responsible for resupplying Egypt and Syria during the war. But did not France, a country with much stronger ties to the United States than the U.S.S.R. do the same (albeit indirectly and on a much lesser scale) by refusing to embargo her military shipments to Libya? And was not the British embargo on arms supplies to all fighting parties observed more strictly toward Israel than toward its Arab neighbors?

Certainly, after the surprising success of the Arab offensive, the Soviet Union established an airlift to Cairo and Damascus and dramatically increased the flow of arms supplies. But to have done less would have incurred major trouble with the Arab world. Even then the Soviet Union hesitated to act positively on some of the Arab arms requests, and cash payments were demanded for every piece of military equipment (Cline and Brewer, 1975). It was only natural for the Soviet Union to give its clients, the Arabs, a chance to reverse the history of their constant defeats by Israel.

Finally, on the local level of the conflict, the Soviets put their airborne divisions on alert and demanded that President Nixon force Israel to return to the October 22 ceasefire lines. Otherwise, the Kremlin implied, it might act unilaterally. This step, more than any other local Soviet action at the time, bordered on irresponsible conduct. It should be taken into account, however, that Moscow was under enormous pressure from

Sadat. [4] In the final analysis, the Soviet failure to keep Brezhnev's promise to the Egyptian president to stop the Israeli encirclement of the Egyptian Third Army may possibly have contributed to Sadat's decision to rely on American rather than Soviet support in search of an Israeli withdrawal.

The Soviet Union was restrained in its support of the Arabs primarily because of two major considerations: first, it had to avoid a direct military confrontation with the United States that could result in a nuclear war; second, for entirely different reasons, both superpowers wanted Israel to survive, but not to win. For the United States an Israeli victory was undesirable because, as Secretary Kissinger felt at the time, another humiliation of the Arabs would make a durable peace less likely. The U.S.S.R. did not desire a decisive victory for either party, but a limited success by the Arabs would reestablish its prestige among them and preserve tension in the region, leaving a major role for the Soviet Union to play in the future.

Thus, on the local level there existed some common ground between the Soviet Union and the United States. Kissinger's negotiations in Moscow enabled the superpowers to act in a semiconcerted fashion. In the Soviet view detente was instrumental in helping "common sense" prevail (Zhurkin, 1975: 299-300). Undoubtedly the survival instinct influenced the policies of both states, but this instinct would exist with or without detente. Detente contributed established lines of communication, better personal acquaintances between American and Soviet leaders, and a common stake in preventing the Middle East conflict from affecting other spheres of the relationship in the period of confrontation.

These positive aspects of detente accomplished nothing more than ending the Arab-Israeli fighting. Beyond that immediate objective, detente did not hinder Soviet efforts to take maximum advantage of the situation by using the October War to isolate the United States, both politically and economically. Detente or no detente, the Kremlin could not resist the opportunity to undermine the international position of its most powerful rival.

On October 9 the Soviet Union appealed to Algeria's Houari Boumédienne and to a number of other Arab and African leaders to support their Egyptian and Syrian brothers in the war against Israel (Laqueur, 1974: 191). But what kind of support did the Soviets have in mind? Presumably not military. The U.S.S.R. at that time was not rushing supplies to the Arab armies because it did not foresee a prolonged confrontation. How then could countries of limited military means and without common borders with Israel influence the outcome of the hostilities? And why Algeria? It would have taken weeks for a significant number of Algerian troops to reach the battlefield, and once there their presence would hardly have made a difference. Was the Soviet appeal primarily symbolic? Or was it directed less against Israel than the United States? It will be recalled that Algeria had hosted the September 1973 Conference of Nonaligned Nations, at which Boumédienne played an important role. By appealing to him, the Kremlin hoped to establish itself as a spokesman for the Arab cause; one that enjoyed considerable popularity among the third world countries. The plan was apparently calculated to ally the communist bloc and the third world against the United States, the only defender of Israel in the international community.

This interpretation is supported by Soviet encouragement of the Arab oil embargo, and later, increased prices for oil. Significantly, the Soviet Union suggested to the Arabs that oil be used as a weapon before the October War (Pravda, 1973b). Immediately after hostilities began, Soviet broadcasts to Arab countries repeated the suggestion, describing it as a means of pressuring the United States and enthusiastically endorsed the oil embargo. Later, in December 1973 and January 1974, Soviet broadcasters (FBIS, 1973) called for continuation of the embargo. After the embargo was lifted, the U.S.S.R. constantly urged higher prices for oil and other raw materials as well as nationalization of oil fields. Lev I. Tolkunov, *Izvestiya's* editor-in-chief and a Central Committee candidate member, advocated (Izvestiya, 1974) "a mutual struggle on the oil front" as a major tool for drawing the Arab states together. Whether or not this advice carried much weight with the leaders of the Arab oil-producing countries, it clearly represented an effort to contribute to Western economic difficulties.[5]

Itself the largest oil producer in the world, the Soviet Union had an economic interest in the increase in oil prices. Even though most of its oil is consumed by an expanding domestic economy, oil exports undoubtedly benefited from the new price structure (more in Horelick, 1975). Nevertheless, the major Soviet motivation was political rather than economic. The oil embargo barely touched on Soviet economic interests.[6] Moscow's appeals to the Arabs to withdraw their investments from Western banks (Tass, 1973) could have proved counterproductive to its own economy, which depended on the stability of the Western economic system for credits and investments.

Despite detente, the Soviet Union felt free to work against the vital interests of the United States, but unlike the military conflict in the Middle East, the oil issue was not likely to cause an armed confrontation between the superpowers. Because Soviet and American strategic interests conflicted over Western access to the Middle Eastern oil reserves, the Kremlin clearly did not feel that detente was applicable.[7]

Currently, Soviet influence in the Middle East is at a new low. The Soviet-Egyptian friendship and cooperation treaty was cancelled by Sadat, who openly opted for reliance on the United States. Moscow's influence in Syria diminished quickly, and even Iraq does not wish to play the role of a Soviet client. Most important, Kissinger's shuttle diplomacy practically excluded the Kremlin from the settlement process.

The Soviets have already initiated attempts to repair the situation or at least to limit the damage. First, they insist that the Geneva conference, where they would have a major voice, should reconvene and be used as the main forum for negotiating peace. Second, despite a violent campaign against Sadat in the Soviet media, the U.S.S.R. is trying to maintain a link with Egypt. This link could be strengthened if Sadat or his successors become disappointed in the good offices of the United States. Soviet military aid to Egypt, which was almost cut off for many months, appears to have been partly restored. President Sadat acknowledged recently (New York Times, 1977) the expected delivery of approximately fifty refurbished MIG-21 fighter aircraft. The Kremlin could also play its traditional Palestinian card. In the past, Soviet support of the extremist demands of the Palestinians was designed to prevent a peaceful settlement. Now that its influence in the area is declining, the regime may decide it can derive certain advantages from the establishment of a Palestinian state with negotiated borders. Possibly it hopes that such a state would become a Soviet stronghold in the Middle East. Significantly, speaking in January 1977 in Tula, Brezhnev expressed (Pravda, 1977g) an interest in finding a formula through talks with the Israelis which would allow for the creation of a Palestinian national home.

Despite its setbacks, the Soviet Union is still determined to fight American influence in the region. Its interest in establishing better relations with the Carter administration did not prevent the Soviet media (Pravda, 1977b) from bitterly assaulting Secretary of State Cyrus Vance's trip to the Middle East. Nevertheless, they claimed that for the sake of detente, the U.S.S.R., while not helping, did not attempt to sabotage the search for peace. However, available evidence indicates that the Soviets simply could not afford to play a major disruptive role, and thus risk further antagonization of the Arabs. Over the years detente barely affected Soviet behavior in this troubled region. The quest for superpower influence rather than a quest for peace dominated Soviet policy toward the Arab-Israeli conflict.

The same holds true for the Soviet approach to the war in Vietnam. As in the case of the Middle East, Soviet prestige in the third world was at stake, and China was again competing for influence. Here, however, Peking enjoyed the advantage of a powerful pro-Chinese faction in the North Vietnamese Politburo. The Soviet media never publicly acknowledged this, but official lecturers were instructed to mention that certain members of the North Vietnamese leadership were connected with Peking, that Chinese military and economic aid was used to pressure Hanoi, and that armed Chinese construction units were allegedly stationed in North Vietnam. The intense Soviet concern over Peking's influence is evidenced by a Soviet propaganda campaign (Pravda, 1975d; Izvestiya, 1975; Krasnaya Zvezda, 1975) launched against the Chinese presence in Southeast Asian countries immediately after the American defeat in the region.

The Nixon administration hoped to persuade the Soviet government to help bring peace to Vietnam. This hope was based on two assumptions: first, that the Soviets wielded tremendous influence in Hanoi; and, second, that they considered detente important enough to use this influence. Both assumptions seem to have been wrong. According to the Kalb brothers (1975), during the May 1972 summit in Moscow, "despite Kissinger's pressure, Gromyko kept insisting that the Kremlin did not control North Vietnam and that Kissinger was overestimating the degree of Soviet influence in Hanoi." Was the Soviet foreign minister playing a game, saying that Moscow did not have the keys to peace in Vietnam? Apparently not. On a number of occasions the North Vietnamese had demonstrated remarkable independence from the Soviet Union: they did not participate in the Soviet-sponsored International Conference of Communist and Workers Parties in 1969, and they had not endorsed the Asian collective security proposal pushed by Moscow since 1969. Of course, the Soviet Union might have halted or drastically curtailed its arms supplies to Hanoi, but such actions could have provoked a serious conflict between the two countries and were politically unfeasible for the Kremlin as well.

Besides, the U.S.S.R. was not really interested in a compromise peace settlement of the Vietnamese conflict. The war was taking a heavy toll from the United States in economic, political, and moral terms. It was making the United States increasingly unpopular in the world, it was dividing American society, and it was encouraging neoisolationist trends within the nation — all to the benefit of the Soviet Union. At the same time, the Kremlin assumed that sooner or later the United States would be forced to withdraw. Who would replace its influence in the region?

Geographically, China is in a far better position than the Soviet Union to dominate Southeast Asia. Since 1970 Peking had been directing a powerful insurgent movement in one country in the area, Cambodia. It was only natural for the Soviets to attempt to counterbalance Chinese influence by building a strong unified Vietnam. The North Vietnamese were careful to preserve an even-handed approach to the Soviet Union and Communist China, but there were reasons to believe that in case of victory Hanoi would shift in the direction of the Soviet Union. The Soviets could more easily provide economic aid to a unified Vietnam and their location would preclude effective control over the area. The Vietnamese also harbored suspicions about their powerful northern neighbor. Without a doubt, all of these factors were carefully calculated by Soviet experts in their reports to decision makers.

In addition, the Soviet Union was trying to encircle China with powerful allies of its own. In August 1971 such efforts resulted in the Soviet-Indian Friendship Treaty. A unified Vietnam allied with the Soviet Union could become a major lever in Soviet discussions with Peking.

Could the Soviet interest in detente outweigh these considerations? As in the Middle East, Soviet and American interests clashed. Detente might restrain Soviet behavior, but not transform it. The U.S.S.R. therefore avoided actions which might have led to military conflict with the United States. The Politburo heatedly debated whether to cancel Nixon's visit because he had ordered massive bombing of Hanoi and Haiphong, as well as the mining of North Vietnamese ports, on the eve of the summit. The discussion ended in the decision to conduct business as usual. On occasion the Soviets asked the North Vietnamese to be more accommodating about certain secondary issues under discussion in Paris. But there was no chance that the Kremlin would give the United States what more than 500,000 American troops failed to accomplish on the battlefield.

Yet another trouble spot where Washington and Moscow found themselves on opposite sides of the fence was Portugal. A NATO member, Portugal was potentially a great prize for the Kremlin, but the risk of provoking a direct confrontation with the West was far greater than in any other case. Furthermore, unlike the experiences of Vietnam and the Middle East, this time the Soviet Union faced not only the United States, but a unified front of West European states as well. Characteristically, the U.S.S.R. did not hesitate to become involved in the Portuguese situation, but it proceeded most cautiously. It apparently determined neither to miss any opportunities nor to overcommit itself.

For a number of years the Soviet Union funded the Portuguese Communist Party. This financial support was increased after the right-wing dictatorship was overthrown in April 1974. According to newspaper reports from Lisbon, Moscow was sending the Portuguese communists about $10 million per month. Other knowledgeable sources (Szulc, 1975-1976: 9) suggest more modest figures of about $2 or $3 million. Regardless of which estimate is closer to the truth, it is clear that the Soviet financial investment in Alvaro Cunhal and his colleagues was fairly substantial.

Interestingly, there is evidence that Moscow first began to use Cubans as proxies in Portugal. Reliable information (Washington Post, 1975) indicates that the Cuban General Intelligence Directorate (DGI) assisted Portuguese leftist officers in establishing a security apparatus and instructed communists on how to organize commando units to terrorize their political opponents. It is a well established fact that the DGI is effectively under the control of the Soviet State Security Committee, the notorious KGB. The DGI is not allowed to initiate any major operation, particularly outside Latin America, without the KGB's approval (Theberge, 1975).

The changes in the composition of the Revolutionary Council following the Armed Forces Movement Assembly, and the replacement of the premier, General Vasco Gonsalves, with the more moderate Admiral Pinheiro de Azevado, deprived the Portuguese communists of any chance to become a dominant political force. The Kremlin accepted this decline in communist power and switched to the more pragmatic tactic of creating an alliance between the socialists and the communists (Pravda, 1975a). The purpose was to assure a greater role for Cunhal and his colleagues in a coalition government and to expel from it the moderate People's Democratic Party, which had become the main target of the Portuguese communists' propaganda attacks. But these tactics did not work either. As a last resort, the Soviets could merely use their media to blame the United States and Western Europe for "interfering" in Portuguese affairs.

Moscow's disappointment was great, particularly because it found itself virtually alone in its support of Cunhal. West European communists, especially the Italian and to a lesser extent the French, felt that Cunhal's crude, straightforward methods and his total dependence on the U.S.S.R. were embarrassing for parties seeking success through elections. On August 6, 1975, *Pravda* carried a major article (1975c) by Konstantin Zarodov, editor-in-chief of *Problemy Mira i Sotsializma,* an international communist monthly published in Prague, but controlled by the Kremlin. Zarodov's article essentially attacked West European reform-minded communists for saying that socialism should not preclude pluralistic democracy and that they themselves intended to respect the will of the electorate. According to Zarodov, communists should not be concerned with winning a popular majority in elections because:

> for them this majority is not an arithmetical concept, but a political one. It is a question of a revolutionary majority which evolves not only as the result of the creation of representatives and elected organs of power, but evolves also in the course of direct revolutionary action by the masses and independent political activities which go far beyond everyday norms of "peaceful" life established in accordance with bourgeois orders.

Zarodov was particularly critical of those communists who would compromise their revolutionary philosophy and strategy for political alliances and electoral activities in order to come to power. "Calls for communists to be 'moderate' should be rejected if communist parties do not want to 'trail along at the back of the movement and not be at its head.' "

Zarodov's article created a major international uproar. It was widely interpreted as a reprimand to communist parties to stop playing at independence and follow Soviet orders. It was also believed to indicate Soviet support for the Stalinist attitudes of Cunhal and his comrades, attitudes even many dedicated communists found distasteful. Zarodov's piece was criticized in a number of West European communist publications, including the French *L'Humanité* and the Italian *L'Unitá*. On September 17, *Pravda* reported (1975b) that Brezhnev met with Zarodov and "gave a high evaluation" of his journal. The message was tough and obvious; Brezhnev was signaling that the Kremlin solidly backed the views expressed by Zarodov.

But exhorting West European communists to line up behind Cunhal and condemning imperialist intrigues in Portugal was practically all Moscow could do under the circumstances. Cunhal probably wanted more Soviet help, but it is not a Soviet tradition to support the losing side with more than symbolic gestures. Tad Szulc (1975-1976: 57) correctly observes that "Moscow never made an overwhelming effort to help Cunhal." If he had appeared to be winning the Soviets would have increased the magnitude of their committment, but the situation was such that they opted for trying to salvage cordial relations with the Lisbon government and the remains of detente instead.

Even during the earlier period, before Cunhal's efforts seemed hopeless, there is evidence to suggest that for the time being Moscow did not consider him and his party indispensable as its main tool in Lisbon. Some Soviet foreign policy experts felt that the Cuban model, which leaves little room for the Communist Old Guard, best suited the Portuguese situation. According to this line of thinking, Cunhal's communist party had little or no chance of rising to power. But radicals among the military, like Castro in the late fifties, might have established a communist dictatorship allied with the Soviet Union, even without the participation of traditional communists.[8] It appeared that, while Moscow admired Cunhal's loyalty to the Soviet line, it might have been comfortable with the left-wing military in much the same way as it is today with Castro, who purged and imprisoned hundreds of prerevolutionary Cuban communists.

The Soviet policy vis-a-vis Portugal ended in total fiasco. It failed to enhance the Soviet position in Lisbon; it barely helped Cunhal (in a sense it was rather a "kiss of death"); and it increased tension in Soviet relations with the West European communist parties. This tension surfaced later in 1976 at the European Communist Conference in Berlin, where the Italians, French, Spanish, and others rejected Brezhnev's doctrine of "proletarian internationalism." The doctrine accorded Moscow the status of first among equals in the international communist movement. Finally, the conflict over Portugal further complicated U.S.-Soviet relations. An influential sector of liberal public opinion, especially among the media, was disturbed by Soviet support of Cunhal, who opposed the most basic democratic freedoms, including freedom of the press. Regardless of the outcome, however, Soviet behavior in Portugal corresponded with the traditional pattern: cautious, pragmatic exploitation of opportunities, without dangerous overcommitment.

The Soviet interference in Angola contributed more than any other factor to a virtual freeze in U.S.-Soviet relations in 1976. For the first time Moscow became involved on a large scale far from its sphere of influence. Secretary of State Kissinger (U.S. Dept. of State, 1976) warned the Kremlin in unusually tough language that "persistent attempts to gain unilateral advantage could not help but damage the state of our relations and, thereby, undermine global stability." On another occasion, Kissinger (1976) deplored "the unacceptable precedent of massive Soviet and Cuban military intervention in a conflict thousands of miles from their shores — with its broad implications for the rest of Africa and, indeed, many other regions of the world." Nevertheless, a detailed analysis of Soviet activities during the Angolan civil war reveals that on the whole the Kremlin followed its usual pattern of behavior.

There were a number of important factors that determined Soviet policy in Angola. As previously mentioned, the U.S.S.R. takes enormous pride in declaring that international trends continue to favor its interests, but the quarrels with Egypt and particularly, the defeat of Soviet clients in Portugal might have suggested otherwise. A victory in Angola on the eve of the Twenty-fifth Party Congress, where the Politburo and Brezhnev personally intended to extol their "great achievements" in the international arena, could be used to impress the gathering. Even more important, the Twenty-fifth Congress was the first event of its magnitude since the beginning of the new relationship with the United States. It would make an excellent vehicle for demonstrating to the lower echelons of the Soviet elite that detente did not inhibit the U.S.S.R.'s ability to pursue an activist foreign policy and to assist its friends. Even though their policies would not be challenged at a party congress, members of the Politburo cannot be indifferent to the views of their closest subordinates, particularly in light of the inevitable political maneuvering that will accompany the coming change of generations in the Kremlin. With these considerations in mind, the consensus concerning Angola was that while detente should be maintained and further developed, for the moment a greater emphasis on diplomacy from a position of strength and international activism would be appropriate.

There was a long-standing relationship between the Soviet Union and the Movement for the Popular Liberation of Angola (MPLA). The KGB started channeling funds to the MPLA in the early sixties (New Leader, 1976: 7). The Soviets' dealings with the MPLA and its Marxist leader Agostinho Neto were not always smooth. In 1973 they even shifted their assistance to one of his chief opponents, Daniel Chipenda (Legum, 1976: 749). But when Neto's fortunes began rising again after the Portuguese revolution, he regained Soviet favor (Washington Post, 1976b). The Goncalves government in Lisbon preferred the MPLA over the other Angolan factions, and had he remained in power, Portuguese troops in Angola would most likely have strongly backed Neto and his followers. But Goncalves was ousted, which might have provoked a chain reaction in Angola. After losing the game in Lisbon, the Soviet regime was faced with a clear possibility of defeat in Luanda.

Several months before Angolan independence, in March and April, the Soviets were providing the MPLA with massive supplies of weapons and ammunition (Washington Post, 1976a). The Portuguese government in no way discouraged this activity. Strengthened by the Soviet military aid, the MPLA managed to push the other two factions — the National Front for the Liberation of Angola (FNLA) and the Union for the Total Independence of Angola (UNITA) — out of Luanda. But soon the military situation changed again and MPLA control of the capital was seriously threatened.

Moscow had to find a way to promote its client's victory without provoking a direct confrontation with the United States. It had some cogent incentives. If the Soviet-supported faction in Angola could win, the U.S.S.R.'s position in southern Africa would dramatically improve. Angola is strategically located so as to put pressure on Western-oriented Zaire in the north and South Africa in the south. Naval facilities on the African west coast could also have appealed to the Soviets.

The success of the venture could easily have turned on an accurate prediction of the U.S. response. As William Griffith suggests (1976 : 342), the Soviet leadership probably "correctly estimated that after the Vietnam War and Watergate, U.S. public and congressional opinion would stop U.S. covert aid to the FNLA and that Washington would not suspend the SALT negotiations or grain sales to Moscow because of Soviet activity in Angola." The Soviets did miscalculate somewhat as to how much the Angolan events would increase U.S. domestic opposition to detente, and to what extent their interference would be used by supporters of a harder line vis-a-vis the U.S.S.R. during the U.S. election campaign. But the basic assumption, that the United States would not intervene militarily proved to be correct. In fact, as soon as Cuban military personnel arrived in Angola in significant numbers, nothing short of massive American supplies to the FNLA and UNITA, as well as encouragement of South Africa to use its muscle to rebuff the Cubans, could have changed the direction of the combat.

Open identification with South Africa was impossible for the United States, both because of its domestic politics and because it would have impelled the majority of African nations to support the Soviet Union. The military options of sending American troops to Angola or threatening Cuba with blockade unless it stopped its intervention were completely impossible politically. The hundreds of America-watchers in the Kremlin were undoubtedly well aware of that. Consequently, beyond the risk that the United States might have a change of heart about detente, the Soviet regime had little cause to worry about specific American responses, either on a regional or on a global level.

Last, but not least, Moscow perceived the Angolan civil war through the prism of its rivalry with Peking. Initially, the importance of the Chinese connection was seriously underestimated. Many observers, both within and outside the administration, tended to view the Soviet intervention in Angola almost solely in the context of East-West relations. Later, another extreme interpretation won wide acceptance: that the Sino-Soviet conflict was the determining factor — to the virtual exclusion of all others — behind the Soviet decision to provide massive aid to the MPLA.

Soviet competition with China in Africa has a long history. By the summer of 1975, the Chinese had established an impressive presence on the continent. They maintained close links with Zambia and Tanzania and were constantly improving their positions in Zaire and Mozambique. Peking's influence could even be sensed in pro-Western Botswana and pro-Soviet Congo-Brazzaville. Finally, guerilla movements in Rhodesia and Namibia were looking to China for support and guidance (Ebinger, 1976: 688). No wonder Moscow became alarmed when the Chinese, in alliance with the FNLA, appeared to have a good chance to assume a dominant voice in Angola. Chinese military instructors were training FNLA troops stationed in Zaire. An FNLA victory, aided by this support from Zaire and China and, more modestly, by the United States, might have redounded mainly to China's credit.

Soviet positions in Africa at the time were insecure. The same insensitivity and heavy-handed approach that had aggravated the Kremlin's troubles with Sadat in Egypt darkened its relations with a number of initially friendly African nations. Its economic assistance was limited, both in terms of quantity and quality: Soviet machinery and consumer goods in particular could hardly satisfy the Africans, who were used to Western standards. The principal benefit Moscow could offer the African states was military assistance. 9 By 1973 it had gained two solid footholds in Africa, Somalia and the Congo (Legum, 1976: 748).

The Chinese also encountered difficulties in Africa, primarily because those states with black regimes needed things that Peking was not in a position to deliver. But China carefully avoided the superpower meddling so distasteful to weak developing nations, and projected an image of belonging to the third world club, which may largely explain its temporary successes.

Considerations other than the Chinese factor influenced Soviet Angolan Policy, such as the rivalry with the United States, and certain domestic pressures. Both motives and opportunity presented themselves to the Soviets: the temptation was too great to resist.

What happened afterward is well documented. After the Organization of African Unity (OAU) called for neutrality, China halted its military assistance to the FNLA and Chinese military instructors went home. Why Peking did not offer more resistance to the Soviet and Cuban interference is open to different interpretations. Possibly, as some observers suggest, the Chinese felt that in the long run they could reap more credit with Angola by complying with the July 1975 OAU decision and withdrawing from the superpower competition there. Another explanation could be that Peking realized that it could not effectively deter the joint Soviet-Cuban venture and preferred to leave the theater voluntarily before being thrown out. The Chinese may also have feared that open cooperation with the United States, and especially South Africa, could have damaged their reputation among the developing countries, their major international constituency. All of these factors probably played a role.

For its part, the United States has done little to stop the Soviets and their Cuban proxies. Congress cancelled covert aid to the FNLA and UNITA, while the Ford administration decided against using tools inherent in the U.S.-Soviet relationship, such as grain shipments and SALT. Thus, the Soviet-Cuban victory became merely a question of time.

The Cubans made a convenient instrument for Soviet intervention. First, they substituted for direct Soviet military involvement, which possibly could have provoked a tougher response from the United States. Second, Cuba unlike the U.S.S.R. and its East European allies, is an influential member of the nonaligned countries movement. Accordingly, many third world states did not perceive the Cuban expeditionary corps as a symbol of neocolonialism. Finally, the large number of blacks among the Cuban soldiers made them more acceptable to the Africans. The Kremlin probably also reasoned that politically the Angolan people would more easily identify with other blacks than with white Europeans. The fact that Cubans were used as Soviet proxies in Angola does not mean that Fidel Catro did not have his own reasons for entering the conflict. There were even reports (Sunday Telegraph, 1977) of occasional friction between the Soviet and Cuban personnel in Angola. But without Soviet financial support, Soviet arms and ammunition, Soviet transport aircraft, and a Soviet political umbrella, Castro's African ambitions stood no chance of being realized. [10]

There is no way of knowing what will be the next target of Soviet-Cuban expansionism in Africa. Among its least likely victims is Rhodesia, as long as the white minority regime is in command, because the Soviet Union seeks quick and easy military successes in Africa rather than confrontations with small, but well-trained and -equipped armies like the Rhodesian one. A Cuban attack against Rhodesia could force South Africa to reevaluate its refusal to cooperate with the Smith regime. Moreover, although such an operation would make the Soviets and Cubans heroes in the eyes of most African governments, it would be counterproductive in terms of other Soviet international interests, especially relations with the West. The unstable political situation in many African nations will probably furnish Moscow and Havana with other, more convenient, opportunities. The Soviet and Cuban wooing of Amin [11] indicates that the most outrageous African government or faction can rely on palpable support, provided it will cooperate with Moscow and Havana against the West. Cuba has established a military presence — ranging from combat units to instructors and technicians — in at least eight or nine black African countries (U.S. News and World Report, 1975: 27) [12], thus setting the scene for new military interventions.

Significantly, Moscow opposed American and British attempts to find a peaceful solution in Rhodesia and Namibia. These attempts were portrayed as "imperialist maneuvers" against the black Africans, who were advised not to cooperate with the Western diplomatic efforts (Pravda, 1977d).

Whether the Soviet Union with Cuban aid will generate more staying power in Africa than it did in the Middle East remains to be seen. Obviously, the Angolan government cannot be as confident as Sadat that the Soviets would comply with a request to withdraw their military personnel without causing any trouble. No African government enjoys international prestige equal to that of Egypt. Nor, in contrast to Egypt, do the African states command military machines that could serve as a restraining factor on the Soviets and Cubans. Finally, only Soviet advisers, technicians, and some pilots were stationed in Egypt, no Soviet combat units. If the Soviets and Cubans should find themselves at odds with their African hosts, this last condition could make a difference.

No matter what step the Kremlin takes next in black Africa, it can be expected to continue its superpower imperialistic diplomacy in the years to come. "The struggle for detente does not at all mean a denial by the socialist states and the international workers movement of fulfilling their international duty to support liberation movements using all forms which may become necessary," declared Rostislav A. Ulyanovskiy (Pravda, 1977a), deputy chief of the Central Committee's International Department.

Assessing Soviet Military Intentions

While there is a great variety of views on the status of the military competition between the United States and the Soviet Union, one basic fact is recognized by all responsible observers: since the mid-sixties, Moscow engaged in a military buildup of unprecedented magnitude. Most experts also agree that this buildup has not been matched by the United States, and that it shifted the military balance to the Soviets' favor. Indeed, Soviet military capabilities have improved to the point where they are widely perceived as equal to American capabilities and in some cases superior to them. Developments of the last decade show that the Soviet regime is no more prepared to accept the existing military balance than to be satisfied with the political status quo. As a matter of fact, these two dimensions of Soviet military-political strategy are interrelated. Growing Soviet global aspirations require a powerful military backup. Even detente, from the Soviet standpoint, was made possible primarily by the growing strength of the U.S.S.R. As Arbatov (1973a), an eloquent spokesman for official policy, put it:

> Recent international events convincingly demonstrate the principal difference between socialism and imperialism in the political utilization of enhanced power. There is no doubt that any change in the balance of power in favor of imperialism would cause not detente, but rather a rise in tensions, would encourage aggressive intentions. On the contrary, a change in the balance of power in favor of socialism serves the interests of the cause of peace and international security.

What does the Kremlin intend to do with its new military power? Is there any limit to the buildup? Would anything short of clearcut superiority over the rest of the world satisfy the Soviet leadership? Finally, is there any hope of convincing the U.S.S.R. that arms control rather than arms buildup best suits its foreign policy interests?

The Soviet regime has always highly respected military power. The Soviet state was born in armed struggle and memories of World War II still strongly color Soviet thinking. The Kremlin does not attribute detente to any fondness for the U.S.S.R. on the part of the capitalist countries, but rather to a shift favoring the Soviets in the balance of power, or, as they call it, the correlation of forces. Their view of the correlation of forces goes beyond military considerations. It includes such components as economic potential, the strength of alliances, and morale. But the role of military power carries extraordinary weight. A prevalent theory (Zhurkin, 1975: 7) holds that by achieving strategic parity with the United States, the Soviet Union forced it to adopt a more realistic approach to relations with the U.S.S.R.

With a few exceptions, Soviet official, academic, and media commentators admit that a nuclear war would turn into a catastrophe of unpredictable proportions.[13] Yet the transformation of the U.S.S.R. from a continental to a global power essentially was based not on economic interdependence with other nations, but on the global reach of the Soviet armed forces, the growing capacity to project power into remote regions. Only in the military sphere can the Soviet regime hope to compete with the United States, which it knows full well.

Experience has taught the Soviets the political value of military superiority in their relations with America. In Berlin in 1961, and in Cuba in 1962, the Kremlin had to retreat without achieving its objectives because the United States enjoyed a superior strategic position. When Khrushchev was forced to take the Soviet missiles out of Cuba, Vasiliy F. Kuznetsov, the Soviet first deputy minister of foreign affairs, at that time on a visit to the United States, warned (Newhouse, 1973: 68) his American host: "Never will we be caught like this again."

A good deal of evidence supports the view that U.S. strategic superiority could not have been utilized effectively during the Cuban missile crisis. Consequently, proponents of this view argue that it did not make much difference that America had more and better ICBMs and strategic bombers than the U.S.S.R. What mattered were the perceptions of the actors. And it is safe to suggest that American strategic superiority during the Cuban missile crisis, even if it was not convertible into a winning capability for the United States, to a great extent influenced the actions of the participants. The Cuban confrontation established that even an illusory strategic superiority results in sizable political benefits. The Kremlin learned this lesson so well that tremendous improvement in its strategic forces followed in the years to come. This buildup was complemented by a simultaneous increase in Soviet conventional, and especially naval, capabilities. James Schlesinger (1974) observed during his tenure as Secretary of Defense:

> The Soviet Union shows that it at least sees no inconsistency between detente and increasing military capabilities. We see continuing increases in Soviet budgets, forces and forward deployments. The Soviet Union is making significant improvements in its strategic nuclear forces and, in concert with its partners in the Warsaw Pact, maintains large and ready general purpose forces.

Some statements by Soviet officials, however, offer comfort to American arms controllers. Arbatov argues, for instance, that "the scientific and technological revolution has pushed military might to a limit, as it were: stockpiles of nuclear explosives in the world are now so large that there are several thousand tons of TNT-equivalent for every person living on the earth." But it has also become clear that this power becomes increasingly less viable as a political weapon. In the words of the well-known military theorist, Clausewitz (Arbatov, 1974):

> It can be said that with the emergence of nuclear missiles "any correspondence between the political ends of war" and the means was lost, since no policy can have the objective of destroying the enemy at the cost of self-annihilation.

There is a striking similarity between Arbatov's position and Secretary Kissinger's statement at his July 3, 1974 press conference in Moscow. According to Kissinger (New York Times, 1974):

> One of the questions which we have to ask ourselves as a country is what in the name of God is strategic superiority? What is the significance of it, politically, militarily, and operationally, at these levels of numbers? What do you do with it?

Unfortunately, it seems that the Soviet regime has rather definite views on what to do with military superiority. Officially, it decries seeking superiority. "The Allegations that the Soviet Union is going beyond that which is sufficient for defense, that it is striving for superiority in armaments with the aim of delivering 'the first strike' are absurd and totally unfounded," Brezhnev claimed (Pravda, 1977g). Yet he added that, "of course, Comrades, we are perfecting our defenses; it cannot be otherwise. We have never sacrificed and will never sacrifice the security of our country or the security of our allies....the Soviet Union defense potential must be sufficient to deter anyone from taking the risk of violating our peaceful life."

Undoubtedly, Soviet defense programs reach beyond protecting the U.S.S.R. and its immediate allies. Its new superpower status has broadened its definition of security. The real problem is, however, that the Soviet government seems reluctant to accept anything less than adequate defense against all possible worst-case scenarios. From the beginning of SALT, Soviet negotiators insisted that they should somehow be compensated for the Chinese threat. Their argument (Pravda, 1977f) runs that the U.S.S.R., unlike the United States, is surrounded by unfriendly states, principally China, and accordingly needs and is entitled to build a larger army than the United States. This makes negotiations about military parity with the Soviets, both in strategic and conventional fields, an extremely difficult and unpromising exercise. What they consider sufficient for their defense would provide them with superior capabilities in most plausible military contingencies.

In recent years there has been a certain change in the Soviet regime's approach to arms control, especially to SALT. Its initial suspicions about substantive arms control measures (which were particularly strong in the military establishment) have been replaced by an appreciation of its value as an effective way to enhance national security. But, this change in attitude has not made the U.S.S.R. more disposed to accept Western strategic doctrines. Such concepts as parity and stability do not play an important role in either determining the structure of Soviet forces or formulating the Soviet approach to arms control negotiations.

Instead, the Soviet leadership acts on the assumption that arms control can codify the military competition, but not abolish it. The Kremlin would probably agree with Edward Luttwak (1976: 6), an able American analyst, who wrote:

> Since the strategic competition is only a symptom of a much deeper and broader political struggle, it cannot be arrested by arms control treaties, nor can it even be seriously constrained. The only effect of limitations on any one class of weapons, or any one mode of performance, is to stimulate new efforts to develop strategic power in directions as yet unconstrained.

This is not to suggest that the Soviet Union is not committed to limiting some kinds of deadly weapons. The government is genuinely concerned by the impact of new technologies on the military balance. Soviet experts have frequently warned that the strategic situation can be destabilized by the introduction of new types of weapons of mass destruction. Another point frequently made by Soviet spokesmen (Pravda, 1977e) is that the development of weapons generally precedes efforts to limit them. Once new strategic weapons are built, the incentive for limiting them is no longer compelling.

American technological superiority must be frustrating to Soviet military planners. Every time the U.S.S.R. has almost overtaken the United States, the introduction of a qualitatively new strategic system once again afforded America some margin. In the late sixties the Soviet military establishment surpassed the United States in numbers of ICBM launchers, only to be confronted with MIRVs and the ABM. Soviet analyses of these developments reflected bitterness and almost paranoid alarm. The United States was charged with seeking a first-strike capability.[14] More recently, the development of American cruise missiles alarmed the Soviets because they lack the miniaturization techniques and sophisticated guidance systems needed to build such missiles. Thus, the Soviet Union is interested in controlling the introduction of new technologies in the context of SALT, but this interest really stems from a desire to rechannel the arms race into fields where the Soviet Union is better equipped to compete with the United States.

Soviet national security policy is not formulated in a fashion that allows for debates about adequate levels of military power. The most important obstacle is probably the disclosure principle, which governs the information flow on sensitive subjects. Only the military, people in the defense industry, and members of the Politburo and Secretariat (and probably not all of them) have access to data about forces structure, deployments, and military R and D programs. Compartmentalization goes so far that as a rule leading scientists working on military research do not know how their findings are applied, and defense industry officials are kept in the dark about how the military employs their products.[15] The famous story about General (now Marshal) Nikolay Ogarkov, who told his American counterparts at the SALT talks not to disclose information about the U.S.S.R.'s strategic deployments in the presence of civilian members of the Soviet delegation, aptly illustrates this secretive syndrome.

But the system is not as irrational as it may seem to an outside observer. It is based on the assumption that every bureaucratic player should mind his own business and not interfere in areas for which he is not primarily responsible. As a result, strategic concepts, the structure of the armed forces, and the attitude toward various arms control neotiations are essentially formulated by professional soldiers and defense industrialists, with little input from defense intellectuals, ivory tower strategists, and skeptics in the legislature or the media.

While a more detailed discussion of Soviet foreign and national security policy formulation will follow in the next chapter, it is appropriate to note here that this process does not favor a focus on such issues as stability and parity. Questions of a different nature probably receive much higher priority. Tom Wolfe (1976 : 157) correctly identifies three basic questions underlying Soviet decisions to initiate new military projects: (1) the availability of technology, (2) the availability of funds, and (3) the importance for Soviet national security.

Changes in the international situation may alter the share of resources available to the military, and so may Soviet domestic developments. If there is any direct connection between Western and Soviet military efforts, it is related only to the introduction of new sophisticated strategic weapons.

A technologically more advanced power, the United States in most cases has been one step ahead of the Soviet Union. When the United States has exercised restraint, it has never been matched by similar restraint on the Soviet side: during pauses in U.S. development of new weapons systems which the U.S.S.R. might have wished to imitate, Soviet funds were simply rechanneled to other avenues of military competition between the superpowers. Since 1965 the United States has added only one new ICBM to its strategic arsenal; the Soviet Union has developed seven (Rumsfeld, 1977: 10).

Soviet military expenditures are extremely difficult to measure. Official Soviet defense figures are low and have remained virtually unchanged over a number of years. Thus, simple comparisons between Soviet and U.S. defense spending are misleading. The Soviet military budget does not include several key expenditures generally considered integral parts of defense spending. Among them are production of arms, equipment and ammunition, military R and D, military components of space programs, military assistance, the cost of 300,000 border guards equipped with modern weapons, and internal security forces also equipped with tanks and aircraft.[16] Furthermore, Western analysts are not familiar with the cost of Soviet military materials (Nove, 1974: 35). Consequently, the most reliable estimates of the Soviet military effort establish not what it costs the U.S.S.R. but what a similar effort would cost the United States.

By applying this methodological approach, two trends can be identified: first, beginning in 1968 the United States reduced its military budget, while the Soviet Union was doing precisely the opposite; second, as a result, by the early seventies the Soviets began significantly to outspend the United States (U.S. Arms Control and Disarmament Agency, 1976: 47, 51). According to the CIA estimate (1977: 5), the approximate dollar cost of Soviet military programs for 1976 was about one-third higher than total U.S. defense outlays. Furthermore, if pensions are not counted, the gap would be in the area of 40 percent. The contrast is especially great if spending on strategic forces is compared: in 1976 the Soviets exceeded the American level by more than three and one-half times (U.S., C.I.A., 1977: 11). Even more striking is evidence (U.S., C.I.A., 1976:) indicating that after 1972, the year of the SALT I agreements, the U.S.S.R. sharply increased its expenditures on strategic forces, so that by 1975 investment in strategic missile systems tripled over the 1972 figures. Finally, new C.I.A. estimates (1976: 16) of the portion of the Soviet gross national product spent for military purposes suggest that it may be as large as 12-13 percent. This estimate looks relatively conservative in comparison to the figures drawn up by Chinese and Soviet dissident sources.[17]

Significantly, the trends in Soviet defense spending indicate that the one strong restraint on Moscow's military programs is neither arms control nor the changing nature of international threats to the Kremlin, but the general performance of the Soviet economy (Calmfors and Rylander, 1976). The CIA study (1976: 16) points out that "because the rate of growth in defense spending was roughly the same as the growth in GNP during 1970-1975, there was little change over the period in the percentage taken by defense." Politically, this observation means that the Kremlin, its international zigzagging notwithstanding, sustained basically the same level of military effort. The structure of this effort was subject to change, but in general the Soviet regime devoted as much of its resources to defense as it could, without totally halting the improvement of domestic consumer standards.

Two arguments are often made to show that the Soviet military buildup does not really threaten the West. First, it is suggested that Moscow has to deploy enough forces to meet challenges from both the West and China. Thus, this argument runs, a significant portion of the Soviet armed forces is not directed against the United States and its allies and should be discounted in calculating the East-West military balance.

In order to do so, however, one has to assume that either the Sino-Soviet rivalry will last forever and the U.S.S.R. will never be able to use its Far Eastern armies in other areas, or, in case of rapprochement with China, the Soviets will proceed with major force and arms reductions. No responsible statesman or strategic planner can rely on either of these two propositions. Consequently, it is easy to envision contingencies when Soviet armies currently deployed near the Chinese border may contribute to Soviet military preponderance over the West. Incidentally, the outcome of the December 1941 battle for Moscow was to a great extent determined by the arrival of fresh Soviet divisions from the Far East where they had been deterring the Japanese. More importantly, the tremendous increase in Soviet military power has not been limited to the Far Eastern theater and was hardly necessitated by the Chinese threat. Soviet conventional forces in Europe were considerably strengthened, both in numbers and quality of weaponry. The growth of the Soviet navy also cannot be explained by competition with the Chinese.

The other argument dismissing the threat of the Soviet buildup holds that the U.S.S.R., as the weaker of the two powers, is committed to reach equilibrium with, not superiority over the United States. Obviously, no one can fathom for sure what is going on in the collective mind of the "enigma wrapped in mystery" known as the Soviet leadership, but the available evidence indicates that the U.S.S.R. will not stop at a level of military power which could be accepted by the West as parity.

First, as was discussed earlier, there is little correlation between Western and Soviet activities in the military field. Second, a concept such as parity seems foreign to Soviet strategic thinking, and SALT failed to change this attitude. Third, the dominant role of the military-industrial complex in Soviet national security policy formulation virtually assures that arguments in favor of continued military growth by the marshals and the defense industrialists will be treated sympathetically. Fourth, growing Soviet global involvement creates a demand for new military capabilities. Fifth, traditional Russian insecurity and suspicion will affect the Soviet determination as to the adequacy of its power. Soviet definitions of parity will probably continue to be based on worst-case scenarios and will therefore be unacceptable to the West. Finally, and possibly the most important of all, previous experience has convinced the Soviet regime that overwhelming military strength pays dividends.

It is difficult, if not impossible, to predict how the Kremlin will use its growing military power. Its innate cautiousness will probably preclude outright military adventures and assure careful calculation of risks. On the other hand, the traditional Russian respect for strength and the newly acquired taste for superpower meddling practically assure that military capabilities will both influence Soviet perceptions of risks and serve political purposes. This means in a passive sense that the U.S.S.R. may assume that the West will not dare support uprisings in East European countries, or in an active sense that it may intervene militarily, directly or by proxy, in areas of political instability from Yugoslavia to Zaire.

III. DOMESTIC DETERMINANTS
OF SOVIET FOREIGN POLICY

In most countries today the previously clear-cut divisions between foreign and domestic political issues are disappearing. Economic challenges make governments aware that prosperity or mere stability at home depends on the international environment. For somewhat different reasons, this interdependence between foreign and domestic policy, only recently appreciated by Western statesmen, was always taken for granted by the Soviet regime. In closed totalitarian societies, foreign policy is integrated into the general political fabric of the system. Changes in foreign policy require domestic adjustments and, similarly, domestic political factors influence behavior abroad. In this context the fundamental question is how far the Soviet leadership can move toward accommodation with the West without encountering major opposition from powerful domestic political interests. To answer this question one must focus on three connected, but separate, issues:

(1) What are the rules and mechanisms of the Soviet decision-making process? (2) Who formulates Soviet foreign policy? and (3) Which essential domestic objectives do they intend to fulfill?

The Bureaucratic Game

To consider the Soviet elite a monolithic body would be a counterproductive oversimplification. Influential forces with diverse, and sometimes conflicting, interests work within the official structure to promote their positions.[18] Bureaucratic debates are the rule rather than the exception, and they are conducted in a different institutional framework and by different rules than under Stalin, or even Khrushchev.

Changes in Soviet society over the last two decades have significantly affected the Soviet elite. While a small group of top decision-makers consists primarily of older men whose political and psychological orientation was formed in the Stalin era, there is a second echelon of the ruling class considerably different from its predecessors. These new members of the bureaucracy are as a rule better educated,[19] more pragmatic and sophisticated, and most important, more secure than the old cadres. The puritanism of the Stalin era is also passé. Fashionable clothes, comfortable apartments and country houses, private cars, expensive dining, and regular trips abroad to learn about the decadent West have become a way of life for this new generation of the Soviet elite.

Some observers argue that these differences between the Old and the New Guard are superficial and do not really alter the approach to substantive domestic and foreign policy issues. After all, recruitment patterns in Soviet society favor those compatible with the current ruling group. Older party, government, academic, military, and cultural bureaucrats decide on promotions; in effect, they choose their successors. Is it not natural to assume that they select copies of themselves?[20] Not necessarily. First of all, each generation is different: society simply does not reproduce the same human material (for more, see Bialer, 1976). Consequently, the actual situation is more variegated than the black and white model of Soviet society. Aleander Yanov, a noted Soviet sociologist now at Berkeley, points out (New York Times, 1975) that the Soviet political scene comprises more than just "heroic dissidence and all-powerful establishment — two basic social strata, the power of one of which is balanced by the sacred rightness of the other."

But the diversity of the Soviet elite does not change one basic fact: however sophisticated and rational this elite may be, it remains the elite of a totalitarian society. Totalitarianism, like any form of government, can be more or less repressive, more or less efficient, more or less sophisticated. But being ruled by the best totalitarian regime in the world still differs greatly from being ruled by a democratic or even an authoritarian government.

A consensus of the Soviet leadership has never been fully reached, even under Stalin. The memoirs of retired officials and military leaders attest to sharp disagreements over policy having occurred in his presence. Stalin's over-whelming authority, however, circumscribed the debates and guaranteed careful execution of decisions by all branches of the government. Following his death, terror and purges became counterproductive to the administration of power and new rules had to be devised (Leonhardt, 1973), which made the formulation of policy much more complicated. Despite the fact that the party apparatus dominates the decision-making process (perhaps to a larger extent than under Stalin when the late dictator sought to preserve his personal power by playing off different party, government, and military agencies against each other), other bureaucracies have become more vocal in promoting and defending their special interests. At the same time, the growing complexity of the policy formulation process has resulted in giving a greater say to lower-level officials, experts, and scientists. Moreover, the structure of the ruling elite itself has changed, and internal conflicts have become institutionalized. A more pluralistic structure has begun to emerge.

Yet recognition of the bureaucratic-political and pluralistic trends in the Soviet Union must be tempered by an appreciation of the nature of Soviet social institutions. The bureaucratic game and the institutional-functional pluralism operate within the framework of a system without democratic traditions or checks and balances. There are certain accepted limits to the game beyond which none of the players dares to tread (see Myers and Simes, 1974).

The Soviet Union remains a state-controlled society. The higher the rung an individual occupies in the official structure, the more dependent he is upon it. The "special benefits" bestowed upon top officials are considerable. Members of the bureaucracy who decide to "go public" with their dissents from the official line must be ready to sacrifice not only their jobs but their whole life style. Naturally, the vast majority of the bureaucracy is reluctant to take such risks. Disagreements among bureaucracies with conflicting interests are generally resolved by mutual gravitation toward the middle position. Participants in the decision-making process tend to avoid outspoken presentation of controversial views.

Each member of the Soviet ruling elite receives his share of state property only so long as he observes the conditions of his unwritten contract with the state, which is usually as long as he retains his position in the party-governmental structure. For the majority, retirement automatically cancels the contract. A few at the top are rewarded with lifelong contracts and some are able to extend coverage to their heirs. In order to remain eligible for the contract, each officeholder must always adhere to the rules of the game. The first rule is that the bureaucratic game is confined predominantly to party and government institutions and seldom breaks out of this institutional framework. Members of the ruling elite can only turn to other members of the same group when they seek support for their positions. Decision-makers appeal neither to "public opinion" nor to their potential constituents among the lower echelons of the bureaucracy. The search for support from within creates a sense of unity and defines the institutional limits of potential conflicts as well.

The Players

Questions abou the identity of the major players in Soviet foreign policy formulation and the relations between them have long intrigued Western analysts. It was frequently speculated that detente had become a subject of controversy between Soviet hardliners and moderates. Usually, military and party ideologists are portrayed as hawks, while economic managers and scientists are supposed to be doves. The lack of hard data makes it difficult to address this question in a responsible, analytical way. As a result, educated guesses are often presented as definite answers. Speculations and extrapolations based on mirror images are sold as reliable pieces of evidence. In fact, the Soviet regime does not mind projecting an image of this hardliners versus softliners game. Soviet spokesmen tell the West that Brezhnev is under enormous pressure from hardliners, and that unless the United States makes important concessions at SALT, the "moderate" Soviet leader could be in trouble. More recently, visiting Soviet officials suggested that if the Carter administration does not stop its human rights campaign, the Soviet military may succeed in its threats to torpedo SALT.

On occasion these rumors reflect reality, but as a rule they should not be taken too seriously. Those who spread them may do it in order to encourage the United States to adopt a more agreeable posture, or to make themselves appear important and well informed in the eyes of Westerners. Or, as happens quite often, the rumors may result from honest errors in judgment. [21] In the closed world of Moscow, rumors are one of the most popular channels of communication, and exaggerations and delusions become inevitable. Consequently, reputable columnists and scholars still argue about who is more hawkish, Brezhnev or Suslov. While there is nothing wrong with such informed speculation, it is not a reliable guideline for policymaking.

Although it is difficult and sometimes practically impossible to learn about positions different Soviet bureaucrats take on all specific issues, there is enough evidence to provide a fairly good idea about some of their views. The evidence more than suffices to draw a reasonably accurate picture of the institutional setup of Soviet foreign and national security policy formulation. The major groups are:

> (1) the Central Committee apparatus (those elements concerned with national security affairs); (2) the military; (3) the defense-related industries; (4) the Ministry of Foreign Affairs, and, (5) the academic-research community [for more details see Myers and Simes, 1974: 24-32].

The relative importance of their inputs varies depending upon the issues under consideration. But in one way or another they usually make their opinions known to the leadership.

There also are other bureaucracies with vested interests in foreign affairs. The economic management may lobby for access to foreign investments and technology. Or, some industrialists may be concerned that an infusion of Western assistance would diminish the need for substantive economic reforms. Ideologists may insist that the ideological struggle and thought controls should be left intact, or even be increased, to balance detente's "subversive" influences on the Soviet population. Party officials from national republics can make a case against greater independence for East European countries, arguing that it could encourage nationalist, if not separatist, movements among their own citizens.

It is hard to evaluate the impact of these outsiders to Soviet foreign policy formulation on important decisions affecting Soviet relations with the West, but on the whole it appears to move such decisions in a conservative direction. Ideologists and local officials, especially from national republics, understandably lack enthusiasm for relaxation between socialism and capitalism. The attitudes of the economic management are probably more complex and contradictory. Its interests, as I have mentioned, work both ways. While it would find new sophisticated technology very attractive, what if the price would be to postpone, if not avoid altogether, economic reforms designed to give management more autonomy and power? It is not an easy choice to make. In the absence of empirical data, one can only speculate that an immediate interest in obtaining new machines and additional funds resulting from Western investments prevails over more remote fears that economic relations with the West may help to conserve the present domination of the party apparatus over the industrialists. Nevertheless, these fears probably qualify the economic management's interest in detente and diminish its otherwise natural zeal in arguing for broader economic cooperation with the West.

If this is indeed the case, it means that there is no overwhelming pressure on the Soviet leadership by interest groups outside foreign policy formulation to perpetuate detente.Rather, support of detente originates in forces directly involved in the international security decision-making process. It may sound paradoxical and ironic to those thinking in terms of mirror images, but available evidence indicates that detente as it has been practiced by the Soviet regime has won the approval of the Soviet military establishment. Marshals and generals have good reason to believe that an improvement in East-West relations will not lead to a slowdown in Soviet military programs. Furthermore, as Malcolm Makintosh (1973: 9) states, "It would appear that the 1972 SALT agreement should also satisfy Soviet military programs. Furthermore, as Malcolm Mackintosh (1973: 9) states, military leaders certainly do not indicate any serious opposition to SALT I or to the Vladivostok accords. Writers associated with the Main Political Administration of the Soviet Armed Forces presumably take exception to them. But even if their disapproval is genuine, rather than representative of an effort to encourage vigilance against the "imperialist enemy," it can hardly play an important role because of their lack of substantive responsibility for the Soviet strategic posture.

Whether or not the Soviet military had reservations about detente, it must have derived satisfaction from formal recognition of Soviet strategic parity with the United States. The agreements allowed the U.S.S.R. superior numbers of ICBM and SLBM launchers and did not rule out the option of developing MIRVs. In addition, the ABM treaty abolished competition with the United States in a field in which the Soviets were less equipped than their rival (Spielman, 1976: 66).

If these reasons were good enough to impress elderly marshals, like then Defense Minister Andrey Grechko and the Chief of the General Staff Matvey Zakharov, they should definitely have convinced their far more sophisticated successors. A striking change in the structure of the Soviet military leadership took place in a little more than half a year. First, Dmitriy Ustinov was selected to replace Grechko, who died in April 1976. Then, after the death of Grechko's closest associate, Marshal Ivan Yakubovskiy, Victor Kulikov (56) was shifted from his position in charge of the General Staff to Yakubovskiy's job as second-in-command at the Ministry of Defense, and was also named commander in chief of the Warsaw Pact forces. Nikolay Ogarkov (59) succeeded Kulikov at the General Staff, and both men were made marshals. They ideally complement Ustinov, who enjoys a reputation for managerial skill, but does not have combat experience. Kulikov is considered one of the best Soviet commanding officers, and Ogarkov is widely regarded as a first-class General Staff strategist. During his tenure with the Soviet SALT I delegation, Ogarkov was respected for his grasp of the issues and his toughness at the bargaining table. "The only problem with Ogarkov is that he is not on our side. I would like to have him with us," a member of the U.S. negotiating team said later.

It is fair to say that the Soviet military machine is now headed by the best-qualified people Soviet society can produce, which contrasts sharply with the previous tradition of relying on elderly ground forces marshals who think in terms of their World War II experiences. It contrasts just as sharply with other branches of the Soviet government and party bureaucracies, which are run by a mediocre gerontocracy.

This praise for the competence of the new Soviet military command should not be interpreted as implying that it will take a softer attitude toward issues affecting the Soviet national interest, or even less, that it will adopt Western strategic concepts. It simply means that the present Soviet military leadership can better realize than its predecessors what is essential and what is not in terms of Soviet military capabilities. Accordingly, arms control agreements, as long as they are favorable to Soviet interests, will be looked upon as benefits, rather than deviations from Marxist-Leninist policy. This position will not put the military on a collision course with the Soviet political leadership. The link between them is maintained by the Defense Council, which is chaired by Brezhnev and includes Kosygin, Podgorny, and Ustinov as members (Garthoff, 1975: 29).[22]

The military's attitude toward arms control seems to be shared by top representatives of the Soviet defense industry. Eight Soviet ministries with prime responsibility for military production are coordinated by the Council of Ministers' Military-Industrial Commission, chaired by Kosygin's deputy, Leonid V. Smirnov. Western technology is probably as attractive to the defense industrialists as to their counterparts in the civilian economy, and an unobliging detente that does not imperil the development of Soviet military hardware cannot jeopardize their interests. Furthermore, Smirnov and his colleagues should not mind if SALT helps to ban ABMs, for which the Soviets possessed no technological capability comparable to that of the United States and allows them to focus on producing MIRVs.

The situation would change dramatically if detente should appear to impose ceilings on Soviet arms development and reductions in the armed forces. Then the marshals and defense industrialists might act in concert to prevent steps damaging to their interests. Since other participants in the national security formulation process are handicapped by a lack of relevant data, the views supported by the military-industrial complex are difficult to challenge.

Significantly, the Central Committee apparatus does not include a department to oversee the military. A defense industry department chaired by Ivan Serbin does not directly supervise the Ministry of Defense. The main political administration of the Armed Forces, while a part of the Ministry of Defense, is considered a Central Committee department; but this institution is responsible for morale and indoctrination (to some extent for clearing appointments), and as mentioned earlier, has relatively little to do with substantive military decisions. Another component of the Central Committee apparatus, the Department of Administrative Organs headed by Ivan Savinkin, also oversees the military establishment to a certain degree. However, it focuses on administration, management, and appointments; substantive military problems are beyond its purview.

Brezhnev's personal secretariat is also hardly qualified to evaluate military proposals. This prestigious group of aides, which sometimes serves as a surrogate staff for the Politburo, includes no military officers of seniority, and possibly none at all (Myers and Simes, 1974: 14-17). This absence of review boards between the Politburo and the military establishment undoubtedly places the latter in a strong position to make its case.

Significantly, in the Politburo itself the military is well represented. Its spokesman there is Defense Minister Ustinov, who was promoted by the Twenty-fifth Party Congress to full membership (Pravda, 1976b). At the time of his election, Ustinov retained the Central Committee secretaryship in charge of the defense industry. Marshal Grechko, then Minister of Defense, was also a member of the Politburo. If one takes into account that Brezhnev was not only awarded the rank of Marshal of the Soviet Union, but also serves as chairman of the Defense Council, and possibly commander in chief of the Soviet armed forces, it emerges that the military-industrial complex had more than ample representation in the fifteen-member Politburo.[23] Brezhnev is known as a good friend of the military, having presided over the military buildup of the last decade. Despite inevitable occasional tension, he apparently gets along well with leading Soviet marshals and generals.

In the Politburo, the military-industrial complex can often rely on the support of the KGB, represented by its chairman Yuriy Andropov. The KGB, which is responsible for maintaining domestic political stability and frequently is used as a tool in Soviet superpower meddling, is not necessarily against detente per se. Unconfirmed reports suggest that some KGB intelligence officers and analysts appreciate the value to the U.S.S.R. of international relaxation. Andropov himself sometimes is associated with this position. Nevertheless, it is difficult to imagine that the KGB would not oppose broader Western interpretations of detente. A greater exchange of people and ideas would give rise to serious problems for the

KGB at home, and an end to the Soviet practice of fishing in troubled waters would significantly curtail its operations abroad.

Much less clear-cut is the viewpoint of the Central Committee International Department, chaired by Boris N. Ponomarev, who also serves as a candidate member of the Politburo. This department deals with West European communist parties, which have an important stake in detente. Consequently, it would probably oppose limited international relaxation. For years, Ponomarev and his associates argued for better relations with socialist parties in Europe. A return to the Cold War would severely hamper the process. On the other hand, reliance on electoral politics heightens the independence of West European communists from Moscow. The aforementioned article by Ponomarev's unofficial subordinate, Zarodov, and writings and statements by other officials in the International Department, convincingly establish Ponomarev's distaste for this trend. Besides maintaining liaison with communist parties, the International Department also handles contacts with so-called revolutionary and progressive movements, which it naturally hopes to encourage. Accordingly, it would be out of character for the department to act as a detente lobby in the Central Committee apparatus. A degree of detente may be viewed as acceptable, even necessary, but not to the extent of perpetuating the international status quo. This argument can easily be identified in Ponomarev's speeches, and in statements by his superior, Mikhail A. Suslov, a Politburo member and Central Committee secretary, who is probably only second in power to Brezhnev himself.

Another important player in the Soviet national security formulation process is the Ministry of Foreign Affairs whose head, Andrey A. Gromyko, sits on the Politburo. Experts often perceive the Foreign Ministry as the strongest spokesman for detente in the Soviet establishment. However, two factors should be considered in assessing this agency's part in the decision-making process. First, the Ministry is charged with implementing, rather than formulating, Soviet foreign policy. The Foreign Ministry's influence is scarcely comparable with that, for example, of the Ministry of Defense. Only one of Gromyko's deputies (there are currently eleven) is a full member of the Central Committee. In contrast, the Twenty-fifth Congress elected twelve deputy ministers of defense (out of fourteen) to full membership (XXV S'ezd, 1976: 315-322). While some ambassadors are full or candidate Central Committee members, so are most military district and fleet commanders.

Second, the Foreign Ministry does not hold a unanimous view of detente. The American and European divisions probably support the improvement of relations with the West with more enthusiasm than others because it improves their operational conditions in Western countries, makes their diplomatic functions both more substantive and intensive, and creates better opportunities for promotions and foreign travel — not unimportant advantages for most Soviet citizens. But those divisions dealing with Asian, African, and Latin American affairs take a dimmer view, although not to the point of opposing controlled and limited detente with the West. Official spokesmen have frequently declared that detente benefits national liberation movements and weakens Western will to become involved in remote regions. Nevertheless, these divisions tend to speak from the standpoint of improving Soviet positions in the third world, and accord lower priority to detente. Consequently, nothing more than a doctrine of limited detente is likely to be promoted by the Ministry of Foreign Affairs.

Finally, the growing complexity and global reach of Soviet foreign policy has resulted in the establishment of a group of research institutes to study different regions and aspects of international relations. Staff members of these institutes prepare papers for the decision-making bodies and often serve as consultants to Central Committee departments, including Brezhnev's personal secretariat. They are usually more sophisticated and broadminded than their bureaucratic counterparts. They also probably have less of a stake in maintaining the Soviet political system intact. A modest relaxation of controls (in the framework of the existing structure) would favor their interests, allowing them more freedom to express their views and a more important role in determining basic international priorities, in the manner of American foreign policy scholars.

At present the decision-makers utilize the expertise of research institutes without affording them a direct voice in policy formulation. Their lack of power is indicated by the fact that no representative of these institutes sits on the Central Committee as a full member.[24] Also, the institutes of the Ministry of Foreign Affairs, like its divisions, are responsible for working on different geographic or topical areas. Consequently, their advice is not homogeneous. All told, the institutes do not form a united front to articulate detente in its Western definition.

To sum up, there are no major bureaucratic players in the framework of the Soviet institute system to present a case in favor of accepting the political and military status quo with the West. Yet a diversity of views and approaches definitely exists in the foreign policy establishment. For instance, there is disagreement over Eurocommunism, especially over the participation of communists in coalition governments. Apparently debates occur about how far the ideological struggle should be pursued, or whether to make minor adjustments in domestic practices in order to promote detente. There is a great deal of evidence that in setting national economic priorities the Soviet leadership must make choices between guns and butter.25 It is reasonable to assume that these choices cannot please all the Soviet bureaucratic players. These are just a few of many subjects under discussion within the Soviet establishment.

The fundamental political outlook of the Soviet elite, however, strictly limits foreign policy debates. Vladimir Petrov perceptively analyzed this outlook (1973: 846-847):

> Its common denominator is a fierce patriotism, a belief in a one-party system, a view that the Soviet Union leads the worldwide struggle against the fundamentally hostile West and that this hostility is predetermined by the conflict between two drastically different socioeconomic systems. The foreign relations elitists further believe that a major war must be prevented; that for its strength and security the Soviet Union depends on its military might; and that in order ultimately to win the struggle it must keep expanding its ties with friendly nations and sociopolitical forces eroding the cohesiveness of the opposing camp. Above all, they believe that the Soviet system is fundamentally "good" and that in the long run this goodness will be recognized by the majority of mankind.

No Soviet leader who wishes to stay in power can challenge this basic philosophy. Speculation that Brezhnev has such an enormous stake in detente that he can overrule the opposition of his associates, ignores both the Soviet leader's personality and the limits of his influence. Despite his enormous power and glory, his new military ranks and decorations, Brezhnev is not a dictator. In Adam Ulam's words (1974: 150-151):

> To be sure no one could mistake Brezhnev for a real or even potential Stalin. In fact, during the past seven years his stature, despite some occasional efforts at a modest personality cult of his own, could not approach even that of Khrushchev at the height of his power, from 1957-1962. Brezhnev, a much less flamboyant man, has been content or constrained to play the first among the equals of the leading group of the Politburo.

On several occasions Brezhnev has suffered setbacks in the Politburo. For instance, he could not obtain a majority on the issue of economic priorities. In 1968, when he negotiated with representatives of Dubcek, he had to take along most members of the Politburo, including those who dissented from his decision to negotiate. In Moscow Brezhnev's talks with Secretary Kissinger in March 1974 were temporarily suspended in order to give the General Secretary a chance to discuss issues under negotiation with other Politburo members (Schwartz, 1975: 180). Similar incidents occurred during other sensitive negotiations.26

During his years in power Brezhnev managed to expel his major rivals, Petri Shelest and Alexander Shelepin, from the Politburo. But he did so by forming a Politburo coalition against his political enemies, rather than by taking unilateral authoritarian action. While Brezhnev is currently dominant, Suslov (frequently thought to be a restraining force on the General Secretary) also enjoys a high political position. He is the only one of three Central Committee secretaries awarded full Politburo membership who owes nothing in his career to Brezhnev. On several occasions he evidently opposed Brezhnev's policies, and it appears that previously Suslov was among Shelepin's protectors in the Kremlin. It was partly becuase of Suslov that it took so long to eject Shelepin from the Politburo (Lugano Review, 1975). According to reliable reports, in 1968 Suslov and Shelepin still favored using political rather than military means to stabilize the situation in Czechoslovakia. Later, in the spring of 1970, there were persistent rumors that Suslov, Shelepin, and Kirill T. Mazurov had challenged Brezhnev's economic performance (Cremona Foundation, 1971: 81). As long as Suslov remains on the Politburo, Brezhnev, despite his tremendous power, cannot take full command. As one observer put it (Cremona Foundation, 1971: 82), "we have in short a Brezhnev dominated regime, but certainly not a Brezhnev dictatorship."

Reports about the General Secretary's deteriorating health encourage speculation about succession in the Kremlin. But, whoever succeeds him as party chief would inevitably find himself in a weaker political position than Brezhnev and more dependent upon the Politburo, at least during his first years in power.

Domestic Constraints on Detente

The Soviets need detente — but can they afford detente? What would its domestic price be? On the other hand, economic cooperation with the West could improve Soviet military potential, help satisfy consumer demands, and strengthen the Soviet position on the international scene. But there are other factors the Politburo must consider carefully if it does not want to be pushed by detente into far-reaching domestic reforms.

First, what would happen to official communist ideology? This ideology cannot be abandoned if totalitarian rule is to be preserved. For decades the Soviet Union has represented itself to its citizens as not just a country but also a cause. Restrictions on freedom, suffering, and shortcomings of the system were explained as necessary in the period of an historic international change from capitalism to socialism. Can the cause of transforming the world be sacrificed in the name of detente? Brzezinski and Huntington (1972) explain why not: "In a broad sense, Soviet ideology requires that the political system move continually toward a predefined goal. To a Soviet Communist stability is illegitimate." It is not a coincidence that Soviet leaders insist that the nature of imperialism has not changed. To say otherwise would in effect leave the country without a purpose. Authoritarian regimes can survive for some time without claiming ambitious goals, but a totalitarian country like the U.S.S.R. must be committed to international change in order to maintain stability at home.

Second, the current regime is more tolerant of internal dissent than any regime in Soviet history. But there are limits to how far the country can relax without risking a collapse of totalitarian structures. There were no dissident movements under Stalin. Khrushchev allowed more freedom of expression and criticism of Stalin's era was encouraged; however, official controls were tight and little criticism emanated from outside the system. Today the situation is quite different. Despite judicial and administrative repression, dissident intellectual and nationalist movements have become an integral part of the Soviet political scene. While many dissidents have been sent to jail and hard labor camps, and others have left the Soviet Union, some of the most prominent oppositional figures, such as Andrey Sakharov and Roy Medvedev, remain in Moscow and continue their outspoken protests. Furthermore, for the first time since the early twenties the regime permitted mass emigration of Soviet citizens. This emigration is still primarily limited to Jews and Germans, ethnic groups who have homelands outside the Soviet Union; a great many people have been denied that privilege. Nevertheless, the whole phenomenon is new to Soviet society and the authorities do not quite know how to cope with it.

Previously no opposition from outside the official system was conceivable. For the first time the Soviet leadership is learning to deal with dissenters, some of whom are protected by international reputations. I believe that from their point of view the Soviets are managing well. They understand that protests make life in the Kremlin less comfortable, but do not necessarily threaten the system. They have settled on exile as an effective way of silencing dissenters without overly arousing Western opinion.

But this is as far as it goes. The Kremlin cannot allow free cultural and informational exchanges with the West without inviting domestic opposition. Leaders like Suslov, who oversee propaganda and indoctrination, are obliged to warn the Politburo about the dangers that detente poses to the purity of communist ideology and the Soviet way of life in general. That explains why leadership calls for intensifying the ideological struggle in this period of detente. In order to justify the continuation of the ideological struggle to the Soviet people, the Kremlin will probably retain some degree of hostility toward the West as an active component of its foreign policy.

A final domestic factor, the Soviet economy, also imposes limits on detente. The regime needs Western credits, technology, and substantial economic assistance in order to avoid making economic reforms. In this sense, economic cooperation with the West represents a force for continuity in Soviet society. However, extensive external economic contacts could create problems for the Kremlin. The regime would have to break a long tradition of self-sufficiency, but dependence upon the West would not seem to be a viable alternative. The Soviets encourage Western investments, but do not allow Westerners to participate in managing enterprises built with their funds and equipment. The party apparatus fiercely resisted the attempts of economic managers to gain some autonomy from party controls; the leaders are therefore not likely to accept foreign participation in operating the Soviet economy. Furthermore, the Soviets have a reputation for being good buyers (in this respect their system of centralization and secrecy is a great help), but poor producers and sellers. Not only are their goods usually of inferior quality, they also have not learned how to promote them. Currently, the Soviet Union is paying for imports with its natural resources, but some of its leaders have criticized the practice; for example, Oil Minister Valentin D. Shashin (Washington Post, 1974) opposed supplying the West with reserves needed by the developing Soviet economy. As an exporter of primary commodities the Soviet Union naturally sides with the third world against the West. The likelihood in the economic field is therefore that the Soviets will have to pursue both economic cooperation with the West and economic war against it.

In sum, crucial domestic factors at work in the U.S.S.R. impose limits on detente with the West. Nothing less than a fundamental transformation of Soviet society could significantly change this situation. Yet, no evidence to date suggests that the Soviet Union is moving in the direction of such a transformation.

Accordingly, there is no reason to get excited over every temporary setback in the U.S.-Soviet relationship. The U.S. government's negotiating skills can help overcome some of the inevitable contradictions between the superpowers. But no one should expect that even the best designed U.S. diplomatic strategy will be able to transform rivals into friends.

NOTES

1. This view is expressed in a responsible and cautious form in Kennan (1976: 674).

2. A similar view was presented by Alexander Bovin (1975), a political commentator close to Brezhnev's personal secretariat.

3. "On September 22, Sadat informed Brezhnev that the war would begin on October 6" (Kalb and Kalb, 1975: 331).

4. Sadat was sending urgent messages almost hourly "to both Brezhnev and President Nixon pointing out that the ceasefire was being systematically violated by Israel" (Heikal, 1975: 256).

5. Curiously, now the U.S.S.R. has some second thoughts about oil price increases. There is a concern openly articulated by the Soviet media that the new financial power of conservative oil-producing nations, most of all anti-Communist Saudi Arabia, works against Soviet interests in the Mideast (Izvestiya, 1977b).

6. There were reports that the Soviet Union was sabotaging the oil embargo by profitably selling oil to the West. But these reports were always dismissed by Moscow as fabrication and slander (FBIS, 1973).

7. The Soviet Union did not take too seriously Kissinger's statement and frequent speculation in the U.S. press about the possibility under certain circumstances of an American occupation of Arab oil fields. Such statements were charged to be nothing more than blackmail (Krasnaya Zvezda, 1975b).

8. Based on interviews with knowledgeable recent arrivals from the Soviet Union and discussions with visiting Soviet foreign policy experts.

9. According to Department of Defense sources, during the last five years Soviet military assistance to African nations amounted to $420 million, while the economic aid only amounted to $165 million (New York Times, 1976).

10. Cuban troops were delivered to Angola aboard IL-62 transport planes for several weeks, flying on almost a daily basis (Washington Post, 1976a). Estimates of the total Soviet cost of the military campaign in Angola vary from $250 million (Washington Post, 1976c) to more than $500 million (Sunday Telegraph, 1977).

11. According to sources described by the Washington Post (1977) as "extremely reliable," there are about 200 Cuban advisers and technicians in Uganda. The Ugandan army is Soviet equipped and included 17 Soviet MIG fighter aircraft (Newsweek, 1977: 35). During a crisis provoked by Amin's attempt to use Americans in his country as hostages, the Soviet media were clearly sympathetic to the Ugandan dictator (Izvestiya, 1977a).

12. There is evidence that the Cuban military presence in Angola is increasing rather than decreasing (Sunday Telegraph, 1977).

13. Several articles carried by Soviet military publications argued that strategic war would mean not the destruction of civilization, but rather the destruction of imperialism. A case was made that the U.S.S.R. could win a nuclear conflict. See, for instance, Admiral Shelyag's article (1974). However, the significance of statements like this should not be overestimated. They originated almost exclusively with political officers of the Soviet armed forces responsible for morale and indoctrination, who are not parties to national security policy formulation. While disturbing views articulated by this group of military commissars cannot and should not be totally disregarded, they do not appear to represent the official Soviet position.

14. Some Soviet writers were warning that a combination of ABM and MIRV could provide the United States with "an illusion of invulnerability" and could

encourage it to place greater reliance on force (SShA: Ekonomika, Politika, Ideologiya, 1970: 123; Listvinov, 1971).

15.   Furthermore, many observers believe that the Soviet defense industry has developed such strong interdependence with the military establishment that it usually tends to act in concert with the military (Shulman, 1974: 113).

16.   Eight defense industry ministries in the Soviet Union have their own budgets. The same is true of the State Committee of Science and Technology, which is in charge of a large portion of the military R and D. Border guards and internal security troops are on budgets of the KGB and of the Ministry of Internal Affairs.

17.   See, for example, Peking Review, 1975: 9-13; and Aleksandr Goltsov and Sergey Ozerov (definitely pen names), 1971.

18.   For an informed discussion of these institutional forces, see Skilling and Griffiths, 1973.

19.   On January 1, 1952, a little more than a year before Stalin's death, only about 68 percent of the secretaries of republican and provincial party committees, and roughly 18 percent of the secretaries of city and district party committees had college educations. By 1967, the figures were 97 percent and 90 percent (Partiynaya Zhizn, 1973). There is no doubt that today, a decade later, these figures are even higher. The same dramatic upgrading of educational levels took place with respect to the Soviet officer corps (Odom, 1976).

20.   This view is articulated, for example, by Conquest, 1975: 486.

21.   I personally had to realize upon my arrival in the United States that quite a few stories about Kremlin inner politics which I heard from presumably reliable sources in Moscow were completely unfounded. Elementary knowledge of the way things are done at the top of the Soviet hierarchy available in Western academic literature proved that some facts I was told could not have taken place. But who has access to this kind of literature in the Soviet Union? This is, incidentally, another argument for being very careful about information received from recent emigres from the U.S.S.R. Jerry Hough is quite right in stressing "the need to become much more rigorous in our assessment of emigre and dissenter evidence" (1976: 94-95).

22.   At the time of Garthoff's writing (1975), Ustinov was still the Central Committee secretary in charge of defense production. He has retained this title since his appointment as defense minister. It is unclear whether somebody else on the Central Committee Secretariat assumed de facto responsibility for supervising defense industrial ministries. If so, this person could have also been added to the Defense Council.

23.   Whether Brezhnev serves at least as de facto commander in chief is still unclear.

24.   Director of the U.S. and Canada Institute Georgiy Arbatov and Nikolay Inozemtsev, director of the World Economy and International Relations Institute, are candidate members.

25.   Heavy penetration of the uniformed military into economic institutions possibly makes debates on this subject less fierce than one would expect. For instance, the military influence was evident even in the central Soviet economic planning authority, GOSPLAN. It was reported that a first deputy chairman of this powerful institution was a colonel-general on active duty (Pravda, 1976a). It appears that at least for the time being the shift of economic priorities from guns to butter ended in failure. The Twenty-fifth Congress, reversing decisions of the previous congress (decisions which were never implemented), once again directed higher growth rates for heavy and defense rather than consumer-oriented industries (XXV S'ezd, 1976: 18).

26. A revealing account of Brezhnev consulting with Kosygin and Podgorny before sending a telegram to warn Somalian leader General Siad Barre of an alleged coup planned against him is provided by Heikal (1975: 90).

REFERENCES

ARBATOV, G. A. (1974) article in Problemy Mira i Sotsialisma 2.
——— (1973a) article in Kommunist 3.
——— (1973b) article in USA: Economics, Politics, Ideology 10.
BIALER, S. (1976) "The Soviet political elite and internal developments in the USSR." in The Soviet Empire: Expansion and Detente. Critical Choices for Americans, Vol. 9. Lexington, Mass.: Lexington Books.
BOVIN, A. (1975) article in Izvestiya (February 6).
BRZEZINSKI, Z. and S. P. HUNTINGTON (1972) Political Power USA/USSR. New York: Viking.
CALMFORS, L. and J. RYLANDER (1976) "Economic restrictions on Soviet defense expenditure — A model approach," in Soviet Economy in a New Perspective. A compendium of papers submitted to the Joint Economic Committee, U.S. Congress. Washington, D.C.: Government Printing Office.
Center for Strategic and International Studies (1976) The Soviet Union: Society and Policy. Williamsburg Conference III. Washington, D.C.: CSIS.
Christian Science Monitor (1975) December 17.
CLINE, R. S. and J. V. E. BREWER (1975) The Outlook for the Middle East. Washington, D.C.: CSIS.
CONQUEST, R. (1975) "A new Russia? A new World?." Foreign Affairs 3, Vol. 53 (April): 482-497.
Cremona Foundation (1971) Analysis of the USSR's 24th Party Congress. Mechanicsville, Md.: Cremona Foundation.
EBINGER, C. K. (1976) "External intervention in internal war: the politics and diplomacy of the Angolan civil war." Orbis (Fall).
EDMONDS, R. (1975) Soviet Foreign Policy 1962-1973. The Paradox of Superpower. New York: Oxford.
Foreign Broadcast Information Service (1973) Soviet Radio Broadcast to Africa (December 4).
GARTHOFF, R. (1975) "SALT and the Soviet military." Problems of Communism (January-February).
GOLTSOV, A. and S. OZEROV (1971) "Raspredeleniye Natsionl'nogo Dokhoda V SSSR." Leningrad: samizdat manuscript.
GRIFFITH, W. E. (1976) "Soviet policy in Africa and Latin America. The Cuban connection" in The Soviet Empire: Expansion and Detente, Critical Choices for Americans, Vol. 9. Lexington, Mass.: Lexington Books.
HEIKAL, M. (1975) The Road to Ramadan. New York: Ballantine.
HORELICK, A. L. (1975) "The Soviet Union, the Middle East, and the evolving world energy situation." Policy Sciences 6.

HOUGH, J. (1976) "Notes and Views, Correspondence." Problems of Communism (September-October).

Izvestiya (1977a) March 1.

——— (1977b) February 26.

——— (1975) August 8.

——— (1974) August 1.

KALB, B. and M. KALB (1975) Kissinger. Boston: Little, Brown.

KENNAN, G. (1976) "The United States and the Soviet Union, 1917-1976." Foreign Affairs 4, Vol. 54 (July).

KHRUSHCHEV, N. (1974) Khrushchev Remembers: The Last Testament. Boston: Little, Brown.

KISSINGER, H. (1976) Speech by the Secretary of State (March 22). Washington: Department of State publication.

Krasnaya Zvezda (1975a) August 5.

——— (1975b) January 12.

LAQUEUR, W. (1974) Confrontation: The Middle East and World Politics. New York: Bantam.

LEGUM, C. (1976) "The Soviet Union, China and the West in Southern Africa." Foreign Affairs 4, Vol. 54 (July).

LENIN, V. I. (1941) Polnoye Sobranie Sochineniy, Vol. 40. Moscow: Izdatel'stvo Politicheskoi Literatury.

LEONHARDT, W. (1973) "The domestic politics of the new Soviet foreign policy." Foreign Affairs 1, Vol. 52.

LISTVINOV, Y. (1971) Perviy Udar. Moscow: Mezhdunarodnaye Otnosheniya.

Lugano Review (1975) 1.

LUTTWAK, E. N. (1976) "Strategic Power: Military Capabilities and Political Utility." The Washington Papers, IV, 38. Beverly Hills and London: Sage Pubs.

MACKINTOSH, M. (1973) "The Soviet military influence on Soviet foreign policy." Problems of Communism (September-October).

Mezhdunarodnaya Zhizn (1974) 6.

MYERS, K. A. and D. SIMES (1974) Soviet Decision Making, Strategic Policy and SALT. ACDA/Pab-243 (December).

NEWHOUSE, J. (1973) Cold Dawn. The Story of SALT. New York: Holt, Rinehart & Winston.

New Leader (1976) January 5.

Newsweek (1977) March 7.

New York Times (1977) February 28.

——— (1976) March 7.

——— (1975) August 21.

——— (1974) July 4.

NOVE, A. (1974) — III, A summary of seminar proceedings in Soviet Naval Developments. Halifax, Nova Scotia: Centre for Foreign Policy Studies.

ODOM, W. E. (1976) "The militarization of Soviet society." Problems of Communism (September-October).

Partiynaya Zhizn (1973) 14 (July).

Peking Review (1975) May.

PETROV, V. (1973) "Formation of Soviet foreign policy." Orbis 3, vol. XVII (Fall).

Pravda (1977a) March 10.   ——— (1976b) March 6.

——— (1977b) February 22.   ——— (1976c) February 25.

——— (1977c) February 19.   ——— (1975a) September 20.

——— (1977d) February 16.   ——— (1975b) September 17.

——— (1977e) February 6.   ——— (1975c) August 6.

64

———— (1977f) February 5.   ———— (1975d) August 4.
———— (1977g) January 19.   ———— (1973a) November 20.
———— (1976a) July 22.   ———— (1973b) September 5.
Problemy Mira i Sotsializma (1974) 1.
RUBINSTEIN,   A. Z. (1974) "Moscow and Cairo: Currents of Influence."
    Problems of Communism (July-August).
RUMSFELD, D. H. (1977) Report of the Secretary of Defense to the Congress on
    the FY 1978 Budget, FY 1979 Authorization Request and FY 1978-1982 Defense
    Programs. Washington, D.C.: Gov. Print. Office.
Sbornik Leninskiy XXXVII (1970) Moscow: Politizdat.
SCHLESINGER, J. R. (1974) Report of the Secretary of Defense to the Congress
    on the FY 1975 Budget and FY 1975-1979 Defense Program. Washington, D.C.:
    Gov. Print. Office.
SCHWARTZ, M. (1975) The Foreign Policy of the USSR: Domestic Factors.
    Encino, Calif: Dickenson.
SHELYAG, V. (1974) article in Krasnaya Zvezda (February 17).
SHULMAN, M. (1974) "SALT and the Soviet Union," in SALT: The Moscow
    Agreements and Beyond. New York: Free Press.
SKILLING, H. G. and F. GRIFFITHS [eds.] (1973) Interest Groups in Soviet
    Politics. Princeton, N.J.: Princeton Univ. Press.
SPIELMAN, K. F. (1976) "Defense industrialists in the USSR." Problems of Com-
    munism (September-October).
SShA: Ekonomika, Politika, Ideologiya (1970): 5.
Sunday Telegraph (1977) February 20.
SZULC, T. (1975-1976) "Lisbon and Washington: behind the Portuguese revolu-
    tion." Foreign Policy 21 (Winter).
TASS (1973) December 2, in English.
THEBERGE, J. D. (1974) The Soviet Presence in Latin America. N.Y.: Crane,
    Russak.
ULAM, A. B. (1976) "Detente under Soviet eyes." Foreign Policy 24 (Fall).
———— (1974) The Russian System. New York: Random House.
U.S. Arms Control and Disarmament Agency (1976) World Military Expenditures
    and Arms Transfers 1966-1975. Washington, D.C.: Gov. Print. Office.
U.S. Central Intelligence Agency (1977) A Dollar Cost Comparison of Soviet and
    U.S. Defense Activities, 1966-1976. Washington, D.C.: Gov. Print. Office.
———— (1976) Estimated Soviet Defense Spending in Rubles, 1970-1975. Washing-
    ton, D.C.: Gov. Print. Office.
U.S. Department of State (1976) News Release, March 23.
———— (1975) press release 231 (May 5).
———— (1973) United States Foreign Policy 1972. Dept. of State Pub. 8699, General
    Foreign Policy Series 274 (April).
U.S. News and World Report (1975) December 8.
Washington Post (1977) March 4.   ———— (1976c) January 6.
———— (1976a) February 6.   ———— (1975) August 10.
———— (1976b) January 16.   ———— (1974) May 28.
WOLFE, T. W. (1976) "Military power and Soviet policy" in The Soviet Empire:
    Expansion and Detente. Critical Choices for Americans, Vol. 9. Lexington,
    Mass.: Lexington Books.
XXV S'ezd Kommunisticheskly Partiyi Sovetskogo Soyuza (1976) Stenografiche-
    skiy otchet, Vol. 2. Moscow: Izdatel'stvo Politicheskoi Literatury.
ZHURKIN, V. V. (1975) SShA i Mezhdunarodno-Politicheskiye Krizisy. Moscow:
    Nauka.